FESTIVE OCCASIONS COOKBOOK

REVISED EDITION

WILLIAMS-SONOMA

FESTIVE OCCASIONS COOKBOOK

REVISED EDITION

GENERAL EDITOR
Chuck Williams

MENU CONCEPTS & RECIPES
Joyce Goldstein

PHOTOGRAPHY
Allan Rosenberg & Allen V. Lott

WELDON OWEN
PUBLISHING

CONTENTS

INTRODUCTION

OCCASIONS

HOLIDAYS

ELEMENTS OF ENTERTAINING

INTRODUCTION

We all love a good party, whether it's a holiday celebration, a birthday bash, an anniversary toast, a family reunion, or an impromptu gathering of friends. This book offers everything you need to throw a memorable, meaningful event.

Set the scene for romance and dream up an intimate meal for two. Deck the mantel and table with wreaths and create a bountiful, old-fashioned Christmas dinner for an entire family. Here, you'll find organizational strategies that will allow your creativity to soar, the fundamentals of service and table decoration that will provide you with a reliable basis for entertaining, and the menus, preparation lists, and recipes that will help you with all the details. Let this volume be your guide, bring your own sense of style and imagination, then relax and enjoy the festivities. After all, it's essential for you and your guests to savor these special moments.

Chuck Williams   *Joyce Goldstein*

Entertaining with Style

First and foremost, *Festive Occasions* can help take the fear out of entertaining. Like a personal party consultant, it guides you through the particulars of planning, leaving you free not only to add your own inimitable style, but also to enjoy the party as it happens. Every bit of information in this book is designed to help guide as well as inspire. The sixteen menus are divided into two sections, one for year-round celebrations, the other tailor-made for holidays. Each menu begins with all the useful and practical information you will need to organize the meal, from preparation tips and decorating ideas to wine recommendations and strategies for cooking in advance. Most of the recipes have been written to yield six servings, but can be multiplied for larger parties.

The menus in *Festive Occasions* have been created and planned by master chef and cookbook author Joyce Goldstein. Cooking methods are simple as well as straightforward and much of the work can be done ahead. While the dishes in each menu are crafted to work together, you can prepare as many or as few as suit your needs. Most of the recipes work for everyday cooking, too, in all sorts of combinations. And you'll probably discover new favorites that will become permanent parts of your culinary repertoire.

When you are ready to entertain, start with the planning strategies presented in this introduction. To find a menu that suits your specific occasion or provides you with a fresh idea, choose from the table of contents. For step-by-step instructions on how to set a table, fold a napkin, arrange flowers and more, consult pages 174–185 at the back of the book. For an explanation of cooking terms and special ingredients, consult the glossary beginning on page 186.

STRATEGIES FOR FESTIVE PARTIES

More than you may realize, the success of a party depends on the guest list. Though it may be stating the obvious, it is essential that your guests enjoy each other's company. To that end, give careful thought to the people you might invite. Consider their interests and personalities and try to select a dynamic blend.

Think, too, about mixing guests in a way likely to encourage conversation. For a sit-down affair with a guest of honor, shuffle the seating between courses so that everyone gets a chance to sit near him or her. For cocktail parties, pay attention to the positioning of the food tables and bar area so that people can gather in comfortable spaces.

To assist you in such deliberations, you might want to keep a party logbook; enter details of each occasion's guest list, seating, menu and other pertinent details. Refer back to it when planning future events and you'll soon gain a reputation as someone who entertains wisely and well.

EXTENDING AN INVITATION

In these busy times, it is important to invite guests well in advance. For a casual dinner, invitations should be extended at least a week ahead. More formal occasions, or parties for which you're inviting people you don't know as well, require the courtesy of at least two weeks' notice. Traditional holidays or gala events such as a wedding, engagement or anniversary call for sending invitations at least one month ahead.

The more formal the occasion, the more it merits printed or written invitations. Formal etiquette calls for your name(s) and the words "request(s) the pleasure of your company," followed by the occasion, date and time, suggested attire and the letters RSVP: an abbreviation of the French request for a response, *répondez s'il vous plaît*. Include your phone number beside or beneath the RSVP if a telephone response is acceptable.

An invitation to a casual meal can be extended orally, but that leaves details open to confusion. A handwritten note, including date, time and an RSVP request, will provide your invitee with a more tangible, accurate reminder. If necessary, call a day or two before the party to confirm.

KEEPING IT RUNNING SMOOTHLY

Observe good hosts or hostesses in action and you'll see that no detail of their guests' comfort goes unnoticed. Becoming a great host or hostess is as easy as making a personal commitment to your guests.

Make a mental checklist to refer to as the party progresses. Keep an eye out for guests' needs. If you see someone monopolizing a conversation, or another with no one to talk to, diplomatically mix up groups. Informal introductions performed by you, rather than by your guests, help break the ice, too.

You may want to consider bringing in help, particularly for large or very formal gatherings. Word of mouth can lead you to reliable firms that supply caterers, wait staff, bartenders and others to share the work or do it all; you'll also find listings in the telephone directory (be sure to ask for and check references). Also consider asking friends to help out.

Whatever happens, don't admit it when things go wrong and don't panic. A recipe you accidentally overcooked will most likely not be noticed by your guests as long as you don't announce the mistake. Remember that a great party usually develops a life of its own, independent of your plans. Relax and enjoy it and your guests will, too.

DECIDING ON THE MENU, SELECTING THE WINES

The occasion itself is your first guide to the foods you might serve. Some holidays have their traditional dishes. Celebrations call for special ingredients and presentations, while less formal foods may be served at a casual gathering. Remember, though, that a few dishes well prepared and served are better than too many that are not well done.

Whatever the occasion, consider which seasonal ingredients might be at their best. Review your guest list and records of past parties to make sure you'll cater to special tastes or dietary needs. And don't serve too much food; guests leave a table happier when satisfied rather than overfed.

If time allows, you could prepare and serve at least part of the menu for a family meal a week or so before the party to practice. A dry run will familiarize you with the recipes and make it even easier to prepare them for the real event.

Once you've selected the menu, the choice of accompanying wines becomes clearer. For every menu in this book, master sommelier Evan Goldstein has provided general wine guidelines and specific varietal suggestions. But some basic rules also bear repeating.

Red with meat, white with fish is the oldest maxim in the canon of wine wisdom.

But today the rule is flexible. Poultry, lighter meats like veal or pork, and richer seafood like salmon or lobster go well with either light red wines or robust whites. Sauces and garnishes also influence your choice, as does the number of courses.

Despite these considerations, the decision need not be complicated. Start with the suggestions found with each menu. Then, seek out a knowledgeable local wine merchant to help you in your deliberations and pay strong attention to your personal preferences. Furthermore, don't feel that you have to pay a lot to ensure quality; good wine doesn't have to be expensive nowadays.

SHOPPING & COOKING AHEAD

The more cooking you can do beforehand, the lighter your workload and anxiety on the day of the party. Many of the recipes in this book lend themselves to preparing in advance. Several days before your gathering, double-check your selected recipes along with the preparation list that appears with each menu. This way you'll know when to shop so that you have the ingredients needed for any advance preparation (meat that requires marination, for example) on hand at the right moment.

No matter the size or type of party, the importance of list making cannot be overemphasized. We recommend that you first read carefully through each recipe and prepare a master shopping list. Divide it into those things you can purchase at the supermarket and those that come from specialty food or wine shops. (Most of the ingredients in this book are sold at good-quality food shops. It is helpful, too, to have access to a reliable butcher and fishmonger.) Check the list against your supplies, checking off the items that you already have. Also list which cooking utensils, pots, pans, baking dishes and so on that are required and check that you have everything on hand. Make another list of linens, flowers, candles, and any other decorations that you might need. Purchase, borrow or rent whatever is necessary to fill in the gaps.

SETTING THE SCENE

The dining room is the most obvious place to set a meal. But try thinking beyond those four walls. A casual party could be held happily in a spacious kitchen, family room or den. For a large, formal dinner, consider clearing an area in the living room for the table. A more intimate dinner may call for a small table by the fireside or near a window. When the weather allows, move the feast outdoors or to a sun room if possible.

Don't forget to clean the house well in advance. Check the guest bathroom for sufficient hand towels, soap and other supplies. Designate an area for hanging coats, too; if the weather is inclement you don't want wet garments thrown on your bed.

TABLES & CHAIRS

For a small party, your dining table and chairs will no doubt meet your needs. As the guest list increases, feel free to press tables and chairs from other rooms into service and use other surfaces as buffet tables. Consider rentals if you don't have enough furniture to meet your needs.

Above all, anticipate your guests' comfort. Try sitting in every seat to make sure there is enough leg room and that chairs are at the right height; move chairs around and provide cushions if necessary.

CHOOSING TABLEWARE

Your selection of tableware will play an important role in setting a style for the party. Ideally, dishware should flatter the food you are serving and play to any theme you might have (such as Italian ceramics for a Mediterranean menu). On a more practical level, however, you need to work with what is available to you, so count to be sure you have enough pieces for the menu you've selected and for the number of guests. Don't hesitate to mix and match patterns. If you do need rentals, call at least a week ahead. You could also borrow dishes from a friend.

FLOWERS & OTHER CENTERPIECES

Well-planned centerpieces enhance a party's festive air. Flowers are the most obvious choice, but all kinds of items can be incorporated, such as shells, ribbons, twigs and leaves. Beautifully arranged seasonal fruits, vegetables or herbs can also make stunning non-floral decorations.

You'll find step-by-step hints on pages 184 and 185, as well as ideas with every menu in this book, for centerpieces ranging from plain to fancy. Always bear in mind that the best ones are low and spread out, allowing guests to see each other across the table.

LIGHTING & MUSIC

A night or two before an evening party, turn on all the lights and look over the setting. If you can, reposition lamps to help define conversation areas.

Candlelight always adds to the ambience and flatters anyone seen in its glow. But be sure to use supplementary electric lights, or the room is likely to be too dark. It's best to use good-quality drip-free candles such as beeswax. Avoid scented candles, which can detract from the food and wine.

Any music you select should serve to subtly enhance the mood. Your personal tastes will certainly play a part in the choice of music you make, but bear in mind guests' inclinations as well. For a very special occasion, you might want to employ musicians or a band. Always keep music low enough that it does not compete with normal conversation.

GIFTS & FAVORS

Special events become all the more lasting when guests are offered mementos to take home. Whether it is a jar of homemade preserves, a bottle of wine with a handmade label, or even a small framed instant photograph used as a placecard, remember that a host gift should not be so grand that it causes embarrassment, requires a special effort of acknowledgment or makes guests feel obliged to reciprocate. Throughout this book, you'll find suggestions for host gifts that you may find useful or inspiring; use them as you see fit.

PUTTING IT ALL TOGETHER

The main elements for a successful party generate from you: the guests, the setting, the accoutrements and the food. This book is designed to help you put them together with confidence and to be a valuble resource for you to rely on. Every piece of information should be treated as a helpful suggestion as there is no such thing as a hard-and-fast rule for entertaining. In the end, we hope you will use our ideas as inspiration to create a festive occasion that is entirely your own.

ROMANTIC DINNER FOR TWO

Whether you are marking Valentine's Day, a special anniversary or some other shared occasion, celebrate with this memorable menu for two. We show it served at a fireside table where the warmth and glow of the flames enhance the mood of romance, but it could just as well be set in a cozy window alcove, on a balcony with a view or by candlelight at the kitchen table.

For this intimate meal, we chose china with a whimsical gold pattern and favorite pieces of silver. Heart-shaped accessories play up the amorous theme, from vases to napkin rings to the gold salt cellars. White flowers such as tulips or roses are simple, yet elegant, and are easy to arrange. Candlelight adds atmosphere as well; a tray of votives fits the scale of a table for two. You could also set small candles in various spots around the room.

Menu

Oysters with Tangerine Salsa

———

*Roast Lobster
with Meyer Lemon Butter*

———

Broiled Squabs in Honey Marinade

Wild Rice

Pear, Fennel & Frisée Salad

———

*Chocolate Pots de Crème with
Candied Rose Petals*

Surprisingly, a dinner for two often entails more advance planning than a larger party. Try to complete most of the preparation ahead of time so you are free to devote the maximum attention to your dinner guest once the evening begins. You can marinate the squabs and make the dessert the night before, then boil the lobster the next day. Check the preparation list on the facing page to help you plan.

If your schedule is tight, serve fewer courses: oysters followed by lobster, or the pear salad followed by the squab. If you are opening the oysters yourself, be sure to do this just before dressing up to avoid splattering your clothes.

WINE RECOMMENDATIONS

Start the evening with a high-quality, lighter-style California sparkling wine or a French Champagne. Continue it with the lobster, or move on to a half-bottle of classic Chardonnay or Sauvignon Blanc, or even a soft Pinot Noir. With the squab, serve a red wine such as Merlot or Côtes du Rhône. With dessert, pour generous snifters of your favorite brandy.

A tray of votive candles illuminates a side table on which an intriguing present awaits opening. Left, casually arranged in a crystal vase on a side table, the delicate white blossoms and curving stems of tulips add to the ambience.

PREPARATION LIST

• The night before, marinate the squabs; make and refrigerate the pots de crème.

• In the morning, boil the lobster, remove and cut up the meat, refill the shells and chill; make and refrigerate the lemon butter.

• Several hours before dining, make the salsa.

• About 30 minutes before, start cooking the wild rice; remove the lemon butter and lobster from the refrigerator. Assemble the salad.

• Before dining, preheat the oven for the lobster; take the dessert from the refrigerator.

• While eating the oysters, roast the lobster.

• While eating the lobster, preheat the broiler for the squabs; dress the salad.

EACH RECIPE YIELDS 2 SERVINGS

A color scheme of white and gold, with heart-shaped accents, creates a very romantic place setting.

OYSTERS WITH TANGERINE SALSA

SERVES 2

You can use more or less jalapeño to taste in this sweet, tart, spicy salsa; but don't make it so hot that it dominates the oysters' flavor. To shuck the shellfish, you need an oyster knife (available at a well-stocked cookware store), or have your fishmonger shuck the oysters and pack them to go on the half shell.

1 small jalapeño (hot green) chili
   pepper, seeded and minced
grated zest and juice of 1 tangerine
freshly ground pepper to taste
12 oysters in the shell
rock salt

Combine the jalapeño, tangerine zest and juice. Add the pepper. Pour into a small ramekin or bowl.

❧ To open the oysters, hold each one in a heavy dish towel with the rounded side of the shell down. Work the tip of an oyster knife into the hinge near the narrow end of the shell; twist the knife to pop open the shell. Slide the knife along the inside of the upper shell to sever the muscle, then pull off the top shell and discard. Loosen the oyster from the bottom shell by sliding the knife under the oyster. Remove any bits of shell debris or sand.

❧ Spread some rock salt in a layer on a serving plate. Place the oysters in their shells on the plate and serve with the salsa. Spoon the salsa over the oysters to eat.

Oysters with Tangerine Salsa

ROAST LOBSTER WITH MEYER LEMON BUTTER

SERVES 2

If you can't find Meyer lemons, mix regular lemon juice and orange juice.

2 teaspoons minced shallot
2 teaspoons finely chopped
  fresh tarragon
2 tablespoons tarragon white
  wine vinegar
½ teaspoon grated Meyer lemon zest
  or regular lemon zest
1 tablespoon fresh Meyer lemon juice
  or 2 teaspoons fresh regular lemon
  juice plus 1 teaspoon orange juice

¼ cup (2 oz/60 g) unsalted butter
  at room temperature
salt and freshly ground pepper to taste
1 live Atlantic (Maine) lobster,
  about 1½ lb (750 g)

*P*lace the shallot, tarragon and vinegar in a small saucepan and cook over high heat to reduce until the liquid is almost totally evaporated and syrupy. Stir in the lemon zest and juice. Let cool, then beat this mixture into the butter. Season to taste with salt and pepper. The butter may be made ahead and refrigerated, covered, up to 1 day.

❧ Bring a large pot of salted water to a boil, drop in the lobster and cook, covered, for 7–8 minutes. Plunge the lobster into cold water. Cut the lobster in half lengthwise and remove the meat from the body and claws as directed on page 188; clean and reserve the body shell halves. Cut all the lobster meat into bite-sized pieces and replace it in the body shell halves. Cover tightly and refrigerate up to 8 hours.

❧ To roast, let the lobsters and the lemon butter come to room temperature; preheat an oven to 350°F (180°C). Spread the butter over the lobster meat, cover loosely with aluminum foil and bake until heated through, about 8 minutes. Serve at once.

Roast Lobster with Meyer Lemon Butter

BROILED SQUABS IN HONEY MARINADE
SERVES 2

The marinade adds delicate flavor and helps the skin turn a burnished mahogany when cooked. Eat rare for the best flavor.

2 squabs, about 1 lb (500 g) each
1 star anise
2 whole cloves
seeds from 1 cardamom pod
one 2-inch (5-cm) piece fresh ginger, smashed with the side of a knife
⅔ cup (5 fl oz/160 ml) light soy sauce
⅓ cup (3 fl oz/90 ml) Scotch or bourbon
⅓ cup (4 oz/125 g) honey
salt, freshly ground pepper, ground ginger and ground cinnamon to taste

To prepare the squabs, insert a sharp knife through the neck cavity of each bird and cut through the back, leaving the breast intact. Remove the backbone, breastbone, cartilage and ribs. Cut the birds in half through the breast. Place the squabs in a glass or plastic container.
❧ Combine the star anise, cloves, cardamom seeds, fresh ginger and soy sauce in a small saucepan over moderate heat. Simmer for 5 minutes, remove from the heat and let steep for 30 minutes. Strain, reserving the liquid. Stir the Scotch or bourbon and honey into the liquid. Pour over the squabs, cover and refrigerate overnight, turning once.
❧ To cook, let the squabs come to room temperature. Preheat a broiler (griller). Lightly sprinkle the squabs with salt, pepper, ground ginger and ground cinnamon. Broil skin-side down for 3–4 minutes, then turn and broil 3–4 minutes on the other side for rare, or cook slightly longer if desired.

WILD RICE
SERVES 2

The nutlike taste of wild rice is the perfect foil for the sweetly marinated squab.

1½ cups (12 fl oz/375 ml) water
salt to taste
½ cup (3 oz/90 g) wild rice
2 tablespoons minced green part of a green (spring) onion
¼ cup (1 oz/30 g) toasted sliced almonds (see glossary)

In a medium saucepan, bring the water to a boil, add the salt and wild rice and reduce heat to a simmer. Cover and cook the wild rice until tender, about 1 hour.
❧ Stir in the green onion. Spoon the wild rice onto individual plates and garnish with the sliced almonds.

What could be more romantic than love letters? Perhaps this is the night to pull out those treasured reminders and read them again together.

PEAR, FENNEL & FRISÉE SALAD
SERVES 2

Served on the same plate as the squab and wild rice, this simple salad also could be served as a first course.

1 firm ripe Comice or other winter pear
1 small fennel bulb
1 small head frisée or 1 bunch watercress
¼ cup (2 fl oz/60 ml) white wine vinegar
2 teaspoons grated fresh ginger
½ teaspoon sugar
½ cup (4 fl oz/125 ml) olive oil
salt and freshly ground pepper to taste

Cut the pear in half lengthwise, remove the stem, core and seeds, then slice thin. Remove the tubular stems from the fennel, reserving any attractive fronds for a garnish, if you like. Cut the bulb into quarters lengthwise and remove the hard center core and any discolored outer portions. Slice thin. Trim the tough stems from the frisée or the watercress.
❧ In a small bowl, stir together the vinegar and grated ginger. Let stand for 5 minutes, then whisk in the sugar and the oil. Season with salt and pepper. Toss the frisée or watercress with half of the vinaigrette and divide between 2 plates. Arrange the pear and fennel slices over the greens and drizzle the rest of the vinaigrette on top. Garnish with the reserved fennel fronds, if using.

Broiled Squabs in Honey Marinade; Wild Rice; Pear, Fennel & Frisée Salad

CHOCOLATE POTS DE CRÈME WITH CANDIED ROSE PETALS

SERVES 2

You can find candied rose petals in gourmet shops, but making your own is quite easy. Be sure to use only unsprayed roses.

FOR THE POTS DE CRÈME:
⅔ cup (5 fl oz/160 ml) heavy
   (double) cream
2 oz (60 g) bittersweet chocolate, grated
2 teaspoons light brown sugar, packed
pinch of salt
2 egg yolks
½ teaspoon vanilla extract (essence)

FOR THE CANDIED ROSE PETALS:
unsprayed rose petals
1 egg white, lightly beaten
½ cup (4 oz/125 g) superfine
   (caster) sugar

To make the pots de crème, place the cream, chocolate, sugar and salt in the top of a double boiler and cook until scalding. Whisk the egg yolks lightly in a small bowl, then whisk in a bit of the hot chocolate cream to warm them. Gradually stir this mixture back into the cream in the double boiler and cook, stirring, over simmering water until thickened, about 10 minutes.

❧ Remove from the heat, stir in the vanilla and pour into pot de crème cups or small custard cups. Let cool uncovered, then chill until cold, about 2 hours or overnight. Remove from the refrigerator about 30 minutes before serving.

❧ Meanwhile, to make the candied rose petals, gently brush each flower petal with egg white, then sprinkle it with sugar. Place the petals on a cake rack and let dry, then use them to garnish the pots de crème.

Chocolate Pots de Crème with Candied Rose Petals

After dinner, retire to a comfy spot and toast each other with a final sip of brandy. Generously sized snifters are perfect for swirling the spirit to develop its aroma. If you are fond of the best, look for Cognac, the classic French brandy. It's labeled according to its age, with the oldest (those that are aged more than 6½ years) bearing the X.O. designation. Each brand has its own characteristics that result from the blender's art.

RITE-OF-SPRING BRUNCH

As the days grow longer and warmer, the advent of spring brings with it a desire to celebrate. This is a good time to enjoy some of nature's finest produce with family and friends at a weekend party. Mother's Day, Easter or any other special event is a good reason for a rite-of-spring brunch.

The season suggests a fresh, simple decorative approach, so we selected dishware in pastel colors for this festive table. For a no-fuss centerpiece, we filled an assortment of clear glass vases and colored mineral-water bottles with colorful blossoms such as tulips, jonquils, Gerbera daisies and anemones. To take advantage of the morning light, this brunch could be set in a sun room or patio, or beside a window with a garden view. If the weather is warm, you might want to move the party outdoors.

Menu

Avocado, Grapefruit & Endive Salad

———

Toast with Sun-dried Tomato Purée

*Spaghetti alla Carbonara
with Peas*

*Asparagus with Toasted Almonds
& Balsamic Vinaigrette*

———

Polenta Pound Cake

———

Red Wine–poached Pears

The brunch menu that follows features ingredients that reflect a blend of the seasons: spring's tender young asparagus and peas, late-winter pears and last summer's preserved vine-ripened tomatoes. Each dish is easily prepared and presented, suiting the relaxed pace of a Saturday or Sunday morning.

The best strategy for a weekend meal is to serve it with a minimum of effort. For that reason, we set the table casually, letting guests help themselves to the first-course salad from a platter placed on a side table. Freshly cooked spaghetti may be presented on individual warm plates, with the asparagus and toasts passed alongside. Dessert also may be offered buffet-style, along with coffee and tea.

WINE RECOMMENDATIONS

With the salad, offer a light-bodied, herbaceous white wine: Sauvignon Blanc or Riesling. For the spaghetti, pour a medium-bodied Italian Chianti or, from California, a slightly peppery Zinfandel. For dessert, try an Italian Vin Santo or sweet Marsala.

Pastel-colored plates highlight the tones of the salad. Left, handwritten postcards double as clever invitations and serve to remind guests of the exact date and time.

PREPARATION LIST

- Up to 2 days before, prepare the sun-dried tomato purée; poach the pears.

- The day before, make the pound cake.

- The night before, prepare the grapefruit segments and vinaigrette for the salad.

- About 2 hours ahead, dice the pancetta and blanch the peas for the spaghetti.

- Up to 1 hour before eating, prepare the asparagus; boil the water for the spaghetti.

- Just before serving, cook the spaghetti; assemble and dress the salad.

EACH RECIPE YIELDS 6 SERVINGS

Several small glass vases can be used to decorate the table. Fill with different types of blossoms to add color.

AVOCADO, GRAPEFRUIT & ENDIVE SALAD

SERVES 6

Have this simple, refreshing salad ready and waiting to be served to guests as they are seated.

FOR THE VINAIGRETTE:

¼ cup (⅜ oz/10 g) chopped fresh
  mint, lightly packed
¼ cup (2 fl oz/60 ml) fresh
  lemon juice
½ cup (4 fl oz/125 ml) fresh grapefruit juice
1 cup (8 fl oz/250 ml) olive oil
3 tablespoons honey
1 tablespoon grated grapefruit zest
salt and freshly ground pepper to taste

FOR THE SALAD:

3 ripe avocados
3 pink grapefruits
4 small heads Belgian endive
  (chicory/witloof)
1 cup (1½ oz/40 g) fresh whole
  mint leaves
¼ cup (⅜ oz/10 g) chopped fresh mint

To make the vinaigrette, place the chopped mint and lemon juice in a small saucepan and bring to a boil. Remove from the heat and let steep for 10 minutes. Strain into a medium bowl. Add the grapefruit juice, olive oil, honey and zest and whisk together. Season with salt and pepper and adjust the sweet and tart ratio.

To make the salad, cut the avocados in half, remove the pit, scoop from the shell with a large spoon and cut into long, thin slices. Peel the grapefruits, remove all the white pith and cut between the membranes to release the

Avocado, Grapefruit & Endive Salad

grapefruit segments. Trim the ends from the endive and separate the leaves. Thinly slice the endive leaves lengthwise. ❧ Combine the endive and mint leaves in a salad bowl and dress with half the vinaigrette. Place on a serving platter or divide among 6 individual plates. Alternate the grapefruit segments and avocado slices atop the greens. Drizzle with the remaining vinaigrette and top with the chopped mint.

TOAST WITH SUN-DRIED TOMATO PURÉE

SERVES 6

Sun-drying is a traditional Italian way to preserve tomatoes. Spread this classic purée on slices of the best-quality bread you can make or buy.

1 cup (6 oz/185 g) oil-packed
    sun-dried tomatoes
1–2 cloves garlic, minced
½ cup (2½ oz/75 g) pitted
    black olives, such as Kalamata
olive oil as needed
½ cup (¾ oz/20 g) chopped fresh
    basil leaves, lightly packed
1 small baguette, sliced, or 12 slices
    fine-grained white bread, halved

*P*lace some of the oil from the sun-dried tomatoes in a small saucepan. Warm the minced garlic in this oil over medium heat for about 2 minutes to remove the bite. Combine the tomatoes, olives, garlic and a little olive oil in a food processor or blender. Pulse to combine to a smooth paste. Stir in the basil. Transfer the purée to a small bowl. Cover and store purée in the refrigerator for up to 2 days. ❧ Toast the bread slices. Spread with purée and serve, or offer the toasts in a basket with the purée alongside.

SPAGHETTI ALLA CARBONARA WITH PEAS

SERVES 6

Sauced with eggs, bacon and cheese, this classic Roman "charcoal-maker's" pasta is a fitting brunch dish. Fresh peas add a touch of spring.

¾ lb (375 g) lean pancetta or bacon
2 cups (8 oz/250 g) fresh shelled peas or
    thawed frozen peas
4 eggs
½ cup (2 oz/60 g) freshly grated
    Parmesan cheese or half pecorino
    romano and half Parmesan cheese
1 tablespoon freshly ground pepper
1 tablespoon salt
1 lb (500 g) spaghetti
2 tablespoons olive oil
additional grated Parmesan cheese and
    freshly ground pepper, optional

*U*nroll the pancetta and cut it crosswise into ¼-inch-wide (6-mm) strips; set aside. Blanch the peas in boiling salted water until tender-firm, about 1–2 minutes. Plunge into cold water, then drain and set aside. Beat together the eggs, cheese and pepper in a large serving bowl. Keep in a warm place near the stove or on a warming shelf. ❧ Bring a large pot of water to a boil. Add the salt, drop in the pasta and cook until al dente, 7–9 minutes. ❧ Meanwhile, heat the oil in a large sauté pan and add the pancetta. Cook, stirring occasionally, until the pancetta is cooked but not crisp, about 5 minutes. Set aside. ❧ When the pasta is al dente, drop the peas into the pasta pot to heat them through quickly. Drain the pasta and peas, add them to the bowl with the eggs, then add the pancetta and most of the drippings. Toss very quickly to combine. The sauce should be a thick liquid. Serve at once. Pass additional cheese and pepper if desired.

Spaghetti alla Carbonara with Peas; Toast with Sun-dried Tomato Purée

ASPARAGUS WITH TOASTED ALMONDS & BALSAMIC VINAIGRETTE

SERVES 6

You can serve the asparagus either hot or at room temperature, allowing you flexibility in make-ahead preparations.

2 lb (1 kg) fresh asparagus
¼ cup (2 oz/60 g) unsalted butter
¼ cup (2 fl oz/60 ml) olive oil
¾ cup (3 oz/90 g) toasted slivered almonds or pine nuts (see glossary)
⅓ cup (3 fl oz/90 ml) balsamic vinegar or to taste
salt and freshly ground pepper to taste

*T*rim the asparagus stalks to the same length. Bring about 2 inches (5 cm) salted water to a boil in a large frying pan; lay the asparagus in the pan and cook, uncovered, until tender-crisp, 3–5 minutes. Remove asparagus and plunge them into cold water, then drain and pat dry. Let cool to room temperature, then prepare the vinaigrette, or prepare the vinaigrette and serve at once.
᪣ To prepare the vinaigrette, heat the butter and oil in a large sauté pan. Add the nuts and stir until hot. Add the balsamic vinegar and, when bubbly, pour over the asparagus. Season with salt and pepper and serve.

POLENTA POUND CAKE

MAKES ONE 9- BY 5- BY 3-INCH (23- BY 13- BY 7.5-CM) LOAF

During baking, this dense loaf cake fills the kitchen with the sweet smell of corn. If you make it in advance, wrap it well in plastic until ready to serve.

1¼ cups (6 oz/185 g) all-purpose (plain) flour
2 teaspoons baking powder
½ teaspoon salt
¼ teaspoon ground nutmeg
1 cup (8 oz/250 g) unsalted butter at room temperature
1 cup (8 oz/250 g) sugar
6 eggs
1 teaspoon vanilla extract (essence)
½ teaspoon almond extract (essence)
grated zest of 1 lemon
¾ cup (4 oz/125 g) sifted yellow cornmeal

*B*utter and flour a 9- by 5- by 3-inch (23- by 13- by 7.5-cm) loaf pan. Preheat an oven to 350°F (180°C).
᪣ Sift the flour, baking powder, salt and nutmeg together; set aside. In a large bowl, beat the butter and sugar together until fluffy. Add the eggs, vanilla, almond extract and lemon zest; beat well. Stir in the flour mixture and the cornmeal and combine well.
᪣ Pour into the prepared loaf pan and bake until a toothpick inserted in the center of the loaf comes out clean, about 1 hour. Let cool in the pan for 15 minutes, then unmold onto a rack to finish cooling. Serve sliced.

Asparagus with Toasted Almonds & Balsamic Vinaigrette

Polenta Pound Cake; Red Wine-poached Pears

RED WINE-POACHED PEARS

SERVES 6

Excellent with polenta pound cake, these are also good on their own, topped with whipped cream or zabaglione. Try the recipe with apples, too.

6 small, firm-ripe Bosc, Winter Nellis
   or Bartlett pears
juice of 1 lemon
grated zest of 1 lemon and 1 orange
1 cinnamon stick
1 star anise
3 whole cloves
1 cup (8 oz/250 g) sugar
½ cup (4 fl oz/125 ml) water
3 cups (24 fl oz/750 ml) dry red wine

Peel the pears and remove the cores from the bottom with a corer, or cut them in half and remove the cores. Set the pears aside in a bowl of water (to cover) mixed with the lemon juice until ready to use.
❧ In a large saucepan or pot, stir together the grated zests, cinnamon, star anise, cloves, sugar, water and wine; bring to a boil. Add the pears, reduce heat to a simmer and poach, uncovered, until a skewer penetrates a pear easily, about 35 minutes for whole pears, 25 minutes for halves. Transfer the pears to a bowl with a slotted spoon. Let the poaching liquid cool, then pour it over the pears. Refrigerate overnight, or up to 2 days. Bring to room temperature, or warm slightly, before serving.

On a side table, a coffee and tea service is framed by casual bouquets of tulips.

GALA BUFFET

On a warm spring or summer day, what could be better than a sunny setting for celebrating an engagement, wedding, anniversary or graduation? A lawn, garden, patio or one or more bright rooms provides ample space for a large-scale gathering. For any of these important occasions, the food, decorations and setting should be both elegant and welcoming. To achieve this, we show one long rented table for seating guests, although of course you could seat guests at two or more smaller tables. For china, we selected blue and white heirloom plates. Place flowers everywhere, in containers of all shapes and sizes.

To make an unforgettable place card, use an instant camera to snap photos of guests as they arrive, slipping the pictures into frames and placing them at each setting. At the party's end, they become charming keepsakes of the event.

Menu

Cheese Platter

———

Shrimp with Oregano & Garlic

Celery, Mushroom & Endive Salad

Fillet of Beef with
Paprika, Coriander & Cumin

Rice & Wild Rice Salad

Tuna with Peppers & Olives

Berry Tiramisù

With this party for twenty-four, a buffet allows guests a greater opportunity to mingle. It is also the most logical way to serve a maximum number of people with minimal effort. The variety of recipes guarantees that there will be something to suit each person's taste. But you could prepare fewer dishes for a smaller gathering, or add recipes from other menus in this book for a larger group.

To make sure that all the buffet items are ready to serve at the same time, read through the preparation list and recipe introductions well ahead of the party. A caterer, friend or family member could provide help if your time is limited, but since all the food is served at room temperature, this menu is easy to assemble in advance.

WINE RECOMMENDATIONS

Offer a selection of both white and red wines. Choose a medium-bodied white with fresh green flavors, such as a light Chardonnay or a French Chablis; for the red, try a fruity Pinot Noir or a Cabernet Sauvignon. With the tiramisù, pour sparkling wine flavored with a little berry liqueur or crème de cassis.

For a large party, set up a liquor bar where guests can serve themselves. To minimize crowding, provide a separate wine and water bar; Left, experiment with various containers for flowers: bowls, champagne buckets, silver teapots, egg cups, Chinese teacups and porcelain tumblers all stand in as vases.

PREPARATION LIST

- Four days ahead, start marinating the beef.
- The day before, sprinkle the beef with salt.
- The night before, prepare the tiramisù.
- Up to 4 hours ahead, make the rice salad.
- Three hours before, prepare the tuna.
- Up to 2 hours before, marinate the shrimp; make the celery salad.
- One hour before, grill the shrimp and roast the beef fillet.

EACH RECIPE YIELDS 6 OR MORE REGULAR–SIZE SERVINGS. FOR A BUFFET PARTY FOR 24 GUESTS, AS SHOWN ON PAGE 30, MULTIPLY EACH RECIPE BY THE QUANTITY INDICATED.

Use an instant photo for a place card that's also a keepsake.

SHRIMP WITH OREGANO & GARLIC

SERVES 6 (MULTIPLY BY 2 FOR BUFFET)

Classic paella-style flavorings season these grilled shrimp. Make extra marinade to offer as a sauce, or simply garnish with lemon. If using wooden skewers, soak them first in warm water for 20 minutes.

36 large shrimp (prawns)
3 tablespoons dried oregano
1 tablespoon minced garlic
1 cup (8 fl oz/250 ml) olive oil
⅓ cup (3 fl oz/90 ml) sherry vinegar
salt and freshly ground pepper to taste
lemon wedges

Shell and devein the shrimp (see glossary); set aside. Warm the oregano and garlic in a small saucepan over medium heat with about 2 tablespoons of the olive oil for about 2 minutes to remove the bite. Remove from the heat and stir in the vinegar and the remaining oil. Season with salt and pepper. Let cool, then pour over the shrimp and marinate for up to 2 hours in the refrigerator.

❧ Prepare a fire in a grill. Position the oiled grill rack 4–6 inches (10–15 cm) above the fire. Or, preheat a broiler (griller). Lift the shrimp from the marinade and thread 3 shrimp on each of 12 skewers. Grill over hot coals or broil until pink, about 2 minutes on each side. Serve with lemon wedges.

CELERY, MUSHROOM & ENDIVE SALAD

SERVES 6 (MULTIPLY BY 2 FOR BUFFET)

A piquant dressing complements the endive's mild bitterness. The dressed salad stays crisp for up to 2 hours.

½ cup (4 fl oz/125 ml) olive oil
¼ cup (2 fl oz/60 ml) toasted walnut oil
¼ cup (2 fl oz/60 ml) fresh lemon juice
¼ cup (2 fl oz/60 ml) heavy (double) cream
2 teaspoons Dijon mustard
salt and freshly ground pepper to taste
2 cups (8 oz/250 g) thinly sliced celery
½ lb (250 g) fresh mushrooms, thinly sliced
5 oz (155 g) Gruyère cheese, cut into long, thin strips
1 cup (4 oz/125 g) walnuts, toasted and coarsely chopped (see glossary)
3–4 heads Belgian endive (chicory/ witloof)

In a small bowl, whisk together the olive oil, walnut oil, lemon juice, cream and mustard until smooth. Season with salt and pepper.

❧ Combine the celery, mushrooms, cheese and walnuts in a large bowl. Add the vinaigrette and toss. Trim the ends from the endive and separate the leaves. Line a large platter with the endive leaves and top with the celery mixture. Or, pour the vinaigrette over the celery, mushrooms and cheese, toss well and use this mixture to fill the endive leaves. Place the filled leaves on a platter and top them with the chopped walnuts.

As an hors d'oeuvre, present a variety of cheeses, breads and crackers. Balance flavors and textures by offering creamy, hard and fresh cheeses such as (clockwise from top right): double-cream Brie, layered Gorgonzola and Cheddar, peppered goat cheese, dry jack, and two varieties of Port Salut. For easy service, place the cheese board near your wine bar.

Shrimp with Oregano & Garlic; Celery, Mushroom & Endive Salad

FILLET OF BEEF WITH PAPRIKA, CORIANDER & CUMIN

SERVES 6 (MULTIPLY BY 2 FOR BUFFET)

The beef, which gets an aromatic flavor from the spice rub, requires 4 days of marination. Serve it rare, leaving the end slices for those who like their meat well done.

1 fillet of beef, about 3½ lb (1.75 kg)
3 tablespoons paprika
2 teaspoons ground cumin
1 tablespoon ground coriander
2 tablespoons freshly ground pepper
1 teaspoon ground nutmeg
¼ teaspoon cayenne pepper
1 tablespoon salt
hot-sweet mustard

*T*rim the fillet of any visible fat and silverskin. Mix together the paprika, cumin, coriander, ground pepper, nutmeg and cayenne. Spread this spice mixture evenly over the beef. Place the meat in a large glass or plastic dish and cover. Let sit in the refrigerator for 4 days. On the third day, sprinkle the meat with the salt.

Tuna with Peppers & Olives; Fillet of Beef with Paprika, Coriander & Cumin; Rice & Wild Rice Salad

☙ To cook, let the meat sit at room temperature for about 1 hour. Preheat a stove-top griddle or a large cast-iron frying pan and preheat an oven to 350°F (180°C). Sear the fillet on the griddle, or in the pan, until brown on all sides, about 6–8 minutes. Transfer the meat to a roasting pan and roast in the oven until a meat thermometer inserted in the center of the fillet registers 120°F (50°C), about 10–15 minutes. Let the meat rest on a carving board, covered with aluminum foil, for 15 minutes, then slice thin. Serve with the hot-sweet mustard.

RICE & WILD RICE SALAD

SERVES 6 (MULTIPLY BY 3 FOR BUFFET)

Subtly perfumed basmati rice and nutlike wild rice combine with a sweetly spiced dressing for this flavorful salad.

FOR THE RICE:
4 cups (32 fl oz/1 l) cold water
4 teaspoons salt
½ cup (3 oz/90 g) wild rice
1½ cups (10 oz/ 315 g) basmati rice
one 2-inch (5-cm) piece fresh ginger

FOR THE VINAIGRETTE:
½ teaspoon ground nutmeg
½ teaspoon ground cumin
2–3 tablespoons fresh lemon juice
½ cup (4 fl oz/125 ml) olive oil or peanut oil
salt and freshly ground pepper to taste

TO FINISH THE SALAD:
½ cup (1½ oz/45 g) chopped green (spring) onions
½ cup (3 oz/90 g) dried currants, soaked in ½ cup (4 fl oz/125 ml) Marsala until soft (10–20 minutes)
⅓ cup (2 oz/60 g) toasted pine nuts or slivered almonds (see glossary)

𝒯o cook the rice, bring 1½ cups (12 fl oz/375 ml) of the water and 2 teaspoons of the salt to a boil in a medium saucepan. Add the wild rice, reduce heat to low, cover and simmer until the rice is tender, about 1 hour.
☙ Combine the basmati rice and the remaining 2½ cups (20 fl oz/625 ml) water in a medium saucepan. Let sit for 1 hour. Then bring to a boil, add the remaining 2 teaspoons salt and the ginger, reduce heat to low, cover and simmer until the rice has absorbed all of the water and is tender, about 15 minutes. Discard the ginger.
☙ To make the vinaigrette, combine the nutmeg and cumin in a small bowl and whisk in the lemon juice. Add the oil and season with salt and pepper.
☙ To finish the salad, combine the wild rice and basmati rice while still warm in a large bowl. Toss the vinaigrette with the rice, then stir in the green onions, currants and any remaining Marsala, and nuts. Adjust the seasoning. Serve at room temperature.

𝒮erve any extra rice salad in a bowl alongside the beef.

TUNA WITH PEPPERS & OLIVES

SERVES 6 (MULTIPLY BY 2 FOR BUFFET)

Make this easy Mediterranean-style salad up to 3 hours ahead to let the flavors mingle.

1 lb (500 g) fresh tuna, cut about 1 inch (2.5 cm) thick, or canned solid-pack tuna in oil or water, drained
2 red bell peppers (capsicums)
2 yellow bell peppers (capsicums)
¾ cup (6 fl oz/180 ml) olive oil
¼ cup (2 fl oz/60 ml) red wine vinegar or more to taste
1 tablespoon minced garlic
2 tablespoons minced anchovy
⅓ cup (2 oz/60 g) capers, rinsed and coarsely chopped
freshly ground pepper to taste
arugula for lining plate, optional
½ cup (2½ oz/75 g) pitted black olives, such as Kalamata, halved
⅓ cup (½ oz/15 g) chopped fresh flat-leaf (Italian) parsley

𝒥f using fresh tuna, place the fillet in an oiled baking dish, cover tightly with aluminum foil and bake in a preheated 450°F (230°C) oven until it is barely pink and still moist in the center, about 8–10 minutes. Remove and let cool. Meanwhile, roast, peel and derib the peppers as directed on page 189. Slice the peppers into thin strips.
☙ Break the cooked or canned tuna into chunks and place in a bowl. In a separate bowl, combine the oil, vinegar, garlic, anchovy and capers. Season with pepper and pour half of this over the tuna. Toss well. Toss the peppers with the remaining vinaigrette. Spread the peppers on a platter lined with arugula, if using, and top the peppers with the tuna; garnish with the olives and parsley.

BERRY TIRAMISÙ

SERVES 12 (MAKE 2 CAKES FOR BUFFET)

This popular Italian dessert gains fresh new flavor from ripe berries. For easier slicing, make and weight the tiramisù the night before. Serve the berry sauce alongside.

FOR THE GÉNOISE:

6 eggs

1 cup (8 oz/250 g) granulated sugar

1 teaspoon vanilla extract (essence)

1 teaspoon grated lemon zest

1 cup (4 oz/125 g) cake (soft-wheat) flour, sifted

6 tablespoons (3 oz/90 g) unsalted butter, melted

FOR THE CUSTARD FILLING:

5 eggs, separated

⅓ cup (3 oz/90 g) granulated sugar

1 lb (500 g) Mascarpone cheese at room temperature

2 tablespoons dark rum or Marsala

1 teaspoon vanilla extract (essence)

FOR THE BERRY FILLING:

4 cups (1 lb/500 g) raspberries or sliced strawberries

¼ cup (2 fl oz/60 ml) dark rum or Marsala

2 tablespoons granulated sugar

FOR THE BERRY SAUCE:

1 cup (4 oz/125 g) raspberries or strawberries

¼ cup (2 oz/60 g) granulated sugar

1 teaspoon vanilla extract (essence)

FOR THE GARNISH:

confectioners' (icing) sugar

12 whole raspberries or strawberries

To make the génoise, preheat an oven to 350°F (180°C). Butter a 9-inch (23-cm) cake pan and line the bottom with baking parchment.

Place the eggs and sugar in the bowl of an electric mixer, set the bowl over hot water and whisk for a few minutes until warm to the touch. Remove from the hot water and beat on high speed with the whisk attachment until very thick and pale and a small amount trailed from the whisk forms a ribbon on the surface of the mixture, about 8 minutes. Stir in the vanilla and lemon zest. With a spatula, gently fold in half the sifted flour, then the melted butter, then the remaining flour. Pour into the prepared pan, tap the pan lightly on the counter to level the batter and bake on the middle rack of the oven until a toothpick inserted in the center of the cake comes out clean, about 30 minutes. Turn the cake out onto a rack to cool. When cool, cut the génoise into 3 layers with a serrated knife.

To make the custard filling, in the bowl of an electric mixer whisk the egg yolks and half the sugar over hot water for a few minutes until warm to the touch. Remove from the hot water and beat on high speed with the whisk attachment until thick, pale and fluffy, about 8–10 minutes.

Mix the Mascarpone with a fork to make sure it is smooth. Fold the Mascarpone into the yolks and sugar, then fold in the rum or Marsala and the vanilla. In a large bowl, beat the egg whites for a few minutes until foamy. Gradually beat in the remaining sugar until soft peaks form, about 1 minute longer. Do not overbeat. Fold the whites into the Mascarpone mixture.

To make the berry filling, mix the berries with the dark rum or Marsala and the sugar and let stand for 10 minutes.

To assemble, place 1 layer of the genoise in the bottom of a 9-inch (23-cm) springform pan. Top evenly with half of the berry filling. Spoon half of the custard over the berries. Place another third of the génoise over the custard and add the remaining filling, then the remaining custard, then the remaining génoise. Wrap the pan with aluminum foil. Weight the cake with several plates and refrigerate overnight.

To prepare the berry sauce, purée the berries, sugar and vanilla in a food processor or blender. Strain out the berry seeds and chill the sauce until serving time.

Immediately before serving, remove the sides from the springform pan and place the cake on a serving plate. Sprinkle the top with confectioners' sugar, garnish with the whole berries and serve with the berry sauce.

For serving the sparkling wine that accompanies the dessert, your most elegant Champagne flutes and a silver cooler add festivity to the celebration.

Berry Tiramisù

TEATIME FÊTE

A teatime gathering in a garden, on a porch or in a sun room can be both lighthearted and serene. Lighthearted because it may celebrate an engagement, a bridal or baby shower, the birthday of a special friend or a family member. Serene because tea is steeped in tradition, evoking an era past.

To complement the freshness of this menu, we used crisp linen tablecloths and napkins, floral-patterned dishware and an abundance of colorful roses and tulips. To encourage guests to mingle and to promote easy conversation, we arranged a variety of seating areas and separate serving tables for the assorted foods and beverages. The cakes, cookies and peaches could be arranged in one area while the sandwiches and their accompaniments could be set on another table, or even in a nearby room. Be sure to provide enough chairs and cushions for every guest to have a seat.

Menu

*Lemon Saffron Tea Bread with Spiced
Blueberry Conserve*

Tuna Pâté with Sun-dried Tomatoes

Pitas with Feta, Walnuts & Aïoli

*Tomato, Tapenade &
Mozzarella Sandwiches*

Jennifer's Chocolate Dream Cookies

Ginger-Orange Madeleines

Peaches in Wine

Long-stemmed Strawberries

The teatime menu for twelve that follows is purposefully light, combining contemporary tastes and old-fashioned dishes. You could offer guests a choice of teas, such as Orange Pekoe or smoky Lapsang Souchong to go with the sandwiches, and a scented Earl Grey or a variety of herbal teas with the sweets. Lemonade and wine spritzers are good alternatives for guests who prefer other drinks.

These recipes are readily adaptable for other meals, too. The sandwiches, cookies and madeleines are excellent at lunchtime or in a picnic basket. Try the conserve and tea bread at breakfast or brunch and the peaches for dessert at any time.

WINE RECOMMENDATIONS

While freshly brewed tea will be poured, wine may also be offered in some form. Spritzers composed of equal parts wine and sparkling water, served over ice with a citrus slice, make a very refreshing drink; try using a slightly sweet wine such as Chenin Blanc or white Zinfandel. With the sandwiches, offer a simple white wine of light to medium body, such as a French Mâcon-Villages or a Sancerre.

If presents are brought for a guest of honor, display them prominently on a nearby chair or table. Left, lace-cap hydrangeas, their pots decorated with pretty ribbon bows, make charming host or hostess gifts.

PREPARATION LIST

• Several months to the day before, make the blueberry conserve.

• Up to a week ahead, make the tapenade.

• The day before, make the tea bread, the madeleines and the cookies.

• The night before, prepare the tuna pâté.

• Up to 4 hours ahead, prepare the pita sandwiches.

• One hour ahead, prepare the peaches.

THIS MENU SERVES 12. FOR A SMALLER GROUP, SERVE FEWER DISHES.

Strewn rose petals add a lovely, festive touch to the tea table. Arrange teaspoons in a small vase or sugar bowl.

A doll-size tea set is displayed as a fitting decoration on a side table.

LEMON SAFFRON TEA BREAD

MAKES ONE 9- BY 5- BY 3-INCH
(23- BY 13- BY 7.5-CM) LOAF

Crushed saffron gives this bread an intense yellow color and subtle perfume. See the glossary for directions on how to crush it.

2 cups (10 oz/315 g) all-purpose
  (plain) flour
2 teaspoons baking powder
1 teaspoon salt
¼ teaspoon baking soda (bicarbonate
  of soda)
½ cup (4 oz/125 g) unsalted butter at
  room temperature
¾ cup (6 oz/185 g) sugar
2 eggs
1 tablespoon grated lemon zest
¼ teaspoon saffron threads crushed
  and steeped in 2 tablespoons fresh
  lemon juice
¾ cup (6 fl oz/180 ml) milk
½ cup (2 oz/60 g) coarsely
  chopped walnuts

*P*reheat an oven to 350°F (180°C). Butter and flour a 9- by 5- by 3-inch (23- by 13- by 7.5-cm) loaf pan.
෫ Sift together the flour, baking powder, salt and baking soda and set aside. In a large bowl, beat the butter and sugar together until fluffy. Beat in the eggs, lemon zest and saffron mixture. With a rubber spatula, fold a third of the dry ingredients, then half the milk into the butter mixture; repeat, ending with the dry ingredients. Mix in the walnuts and pour into the prepared loaf pan.
෫ Bake on the middle rack of the oven until a skewer inserted in the center of the loaf comes out clean, about 1 hour. Let cool in the pan on a rack for 10 minutes, then turn out onto the rack to cool completely. Wrap the bread in plastic and let sit overnight to mellow. Slice thinly to serve.

SPICED BLUEBERRY CONSERVE

MAKES ABOUT 5 CUPS (40 OZ/1.2 KG)

Sweet spices, citrus zest and a splash of cider vinegar contribute extra flavor and tang to this thick-textured preserve.

4 cups (1 lb/500 g) fresh or thawed
  frozen whole blueberries
3 cups (1½ lb/750 g) sugar
½ teaspoon ground cinnamon
¼ teaspoon ground allspice
¼ cup (2 fl oz/60 ml) cider vinegar
¼ cup (2 fl oz/60 ml) fresh lemon juice
grated zest of 1 lemon
grated zest of 1 orange, optional

*I*n a large, heavy enameled or stainless-steel pot, combine all of the ingredients and bring to a boil. Reduce the heat and simmer, uncovered and stirring occasionally, until thickened, about 25 minutes. This jam sets up fast; it is done when a teaspoonful is still a little runny when dropped on a chilled plate.
෫ Pour into 5 hot sterilized 1-cup (8–fl oz/250-ml) canning jars, leaving about ½ inch (12 mm) of head space, then seal the jars. Process in a hot-water bath for 10 minutes (see Canning, page 186), or store in the refrigerator for up to 3 months.

*Lemon Saffron Tea Bread;
Spiced Blueberry Conserve*

TUNA PÂTÉ WITH SUN-DRIED TOMATOES

MAKES ABOUT 24 OPEN-FACED SANDWICHES

Sun-dried tomatoes, red onion and fresh basil brighten the taste and color of this simple spread. If you wish to make your own country bread, see the recipe on page 176.

FOR THE TUNA PÂTÉ:

1 lb (500 g) fresh tuna, cut about 1 inch (2.5 cm) thick, or canned solid-pack tuna in oil or water, drained
¼ cup (2 fl oz/60 ml) fresh lemon juice
⅔ cup (3 oz/90 g) finely chopped red (Spanish) onion
about 1 cup (8 fl oz/250 ml) mayonnaise
½ cup (4 oz/125 g) finely chopped sun-dried tomatoes
¼ cup (⅜ oz/10 g) chopped fresh basil
salt and freshly ground pepper to taste

FOR THE SANDWICHES:

1 cup (1½ oz/40 g) lightly packed fresh basil leaves
¼ cup (1 oz/30 g) freshly grated Parmesan cheese
3 tablespoons pine nuts
2 cloves garlic
½ cup (4 fl oz/125 ml) olive oil
12 large slices focaccia or country bread
paper-thin lemon slices

To make the pâté: If using fresh tuna, place the fillet in an oiled baking dish, cover tightly with aluminum foil and bake in a preheated 450°F (230°C) oven until it is barely pink and still moist in the center, about 8–10 minutes. Remove and let cool. Mash the cooked

Tuna Pâté with Sun-dried Tomatoes;
Tomato, Tapenade & Mozzarella Sandwiches;
Pitas with Feta, Walnuts & Aïoli

or canned tuna with a fork or pulse briefly in a food processor. Transfer to a bowl and add the lemon juice, red onion, mayonnaise, sun-dried tomatoes and chopped basil and mix until you have a spreadable consistency. Season with salt and pepper. Cover and refrigerate until ready to use, up to 8 hours.

❧ To make the sandwiches, process the basil leaves, cheese, pine nuts, garlic and oil in a blender or food processor until smooth. Cut the focaccia or country bread slices into small squares, then top with the basil mixture and the tuna pâté. Serve open-faced. Garnish with lemon.

PITAS WITH FETA, WALNUTS & AÏOLI

MAKES 12 PITA SANDWICH HALVES, OR 24 MINI PITAS

A vivid combination of tastes, textures and colors goes into these sandwiches. If made ahead, cover them with a clean, damp cloth to keep the pita moist.

6 pita bread rounds, or 24 mini pitas
about ½ cup (4 fl oz/125 ml) aïoli (recipe on page 174)
24 large watercress sprigs
36 large fresh mint leaves
1 lb (500 g) feta cheese, cut into 12 thin slices
1½ cups (6 oz/185 g) chopped walnuts
6 red bell peppers (capsicums), roasted, peeled and chopped (see glossary)

Cut the pita rounds in half and carefully open the pockets (for mini pitas, slice off the top third of the pita rounds and open the pocket). Spread the aïoli inside the pitas. Into each sandwich, tuck even amounts of watercress, mint, feta, walnuts and bell peppers. If desired, cover and refrigerate the sandwiches until ready to serve, up to 4 hours.

TOMATO, TAPENADE & MOZZARELLA SANDWICHES

MAKES 24 SMALL SANDWICHES

Tapenade, a pungent niçoise olive spread, can be made ahead and refrigerated for up to 1 week. A recipe for homemade baguettes appears on page 176.

FOR THE TAPENADE:

1 cup (5 oz/155 g) pitted green or black niçoise olives
2 tablespoons chopped rinsed capers
1 tablespoon minced garlic
2 teaspoons chopped anchovies
½ teaspoon freshly ground pepper
1 teaspoon grated orange or lemon zest
pinch of red pepper flakes, optional
4–6 tablespoons (2–3 fl oz/60–90 ml) olive oil

FOR THE SANDWICHES:

1 long baguette (about 1 lb/500 g)
6–8 plum (Roma) tomatoes, sliced
two 8-ounce (250-g) balls fresh mozzarella cheese, sliced
24 arugula leaves

To make the tapenade, combine the olives, capers, garlic, anchovies, ground pepper, zest and optional red pepper flakes in a food processor or blender. Purée, pouring in enough oil to make a thick spread. Makes 1 cup (8 fl oz/250 ml).

❧ To make the sandwiches, cut the baguette in half lengthwise, then cut each half into 12 diagonal slices. Spread each slice with tapenade. Top each piece equally with sliced tomatoes, sliced mozzarella cheese and an arugula leaf. Serve open-faced.

JENNIFER'S CHOCOLATE DREAM COOKIES

MAKES 48 COOKIES

Light and crackly on the outside, soft and chewy within, these cookies are reminiscent of good chocolate fudge.

2 cups (10 oz/315 g) all-purpose
　(plain) flour
¾ cup (3 oz/90 g) sifted cocoa
2 teaspoons baking powder
1 teaspoon salt
1 cup (8 oz/250 g) unsalted butter at
　room temperature
1 cup (7 oz/220 g) dark brown
　sugar, packed
1 cup (8 oz/250 g) granulated sugar
2 teaspoons vanilla extract (essence)
2 eggs
6 oz (185 g) bittersweet chocolate,
　coarsely chopped, or bittersweet
　chocolate chips

Preheat an oven to 325°F (170°C). Line 2 baking sheets with baking parchment. Sift the flour, cocoa, baking powder and salt together into a medium bowl.
❧ In a large bowl, beat the butter, brown sugar and granulated sugar together until fluffy. Add the vanilla and eggs and beat well. Stir in the flour-cocoa mixture, then fold in the chocolate chunks.
❧ Drop the cookie dough by the tablespoonful onto the prepared baking sheets. Bake until the cookies are puffed and set but still chewy in the middle, about 8–10 minutes. Let cool on racks. If made ahead, store in a plastic container until ready to use.

GINGER-ORANGE MADELEINES

MAKES 36 MADELEINES

These delicate little sponge cakes gain subtle flavor from orange zest and candied ginger. If you don't have enough madeleine pans, bake them in batches.

3 eggs
2 egg yolks
pinch of salt
¾ cup (6 oz/185 g) granulated sugar
2 tablespoons grated orange zest soaked
　in 3 tablespoons orange juice
1¼ cups (5 oz/155 g) sifted all-purpose
　(plain) flour
¼ cup (1 oz/30 g) finely chopped
　candied ginger
½ cup (4 oz/125 g) plus 2 tablespoons
　unsalted butter, clarified (see glossary)
confectioners' (icing) sugar for sprinkling

Preheat an oven to 350°F (180°C). Butter and lightly flour 4 standard madeleine pans (or fewer, if necessary).
❧ Place the whole eggs, egg yolks and granulated sugar together in the bowl of an electric mixer, set the bowl over hot water and whisk for a few minutes until warm to the touch. Remove from the hot water, add the salt and beat on high speed until the mixture is very thick and pale. Add the orange zest and juice and beat well. Sift the flour over the batter and fold it in, then fold in the ginger. Finally, fold in the butter a little at a time. Fill the molds two-thirds of the way full with batter, then bake until golden, about 15 minutes.
❧ Gently loosen the sides of the madeleines from the molds and turn them out onto a rack. Sprinkle the ribbed sides with confectioners' sugar while still warm.

If you want to offer a selection of teas, provide a few individual pots and tea strainers so that a guest can pour his or her own cupful.

Ginger-Orange Madeleines;
Jennifer's Chocolate Dream Cookies

PEACHES IN WINE

SERVES 12

For such elegant results, the preparation of this light dessert could not be simpler. Nectarines also work well.

12 ripe peaches
4 cups (32 fl oz/1 l) fruity white wine
  such as Asti Spumante, Moscato or
  Riesling, or a light, fruity red wine
  such as Lambrusco or Beaujolais
1 cup (8 oz/250 g) sugar

Bring a large pot of water to a boil. Drop in a few peaches at a time for 5 seconds to loosen the skin. Lift out with a slotted spoon, let cool briefly, then peel. Cut the peaches in half and remove the pits.

Combine the wine and sugar in an attractive glass bowl; stir until the sugar dissolves. Slice the peaches and place them in the wine. Chill for 1 hour, then serve.

Refreshing lemonade, offered in tall glasses over ice, is a delicious beverage to offer in addition to tea.

Peaches in Wine

AL FRESCO LUNCH

Warm weather brings the irresistible urge to eat outdoors. While that usually means a casual barbecue or picnic, you might want to try a sit-down, open-air lunch. You'll find plenty of reasons to serve this menu: summer holidays, birthdays, end-of-the-weekend send-offs, or simply just to enjoy the weather.

A beachside getaway is an ideal location, with the table set up in or near the sand, but this menu is equally appropriate served on a deck or even in a sunny room at home. To contrast with the casual outdoor setting, we dressed the table with good china, silver, crystal, linens, and folded the napkins into bishop's hats (page 183). Director's chairs provided informal seating. Taking advantage of the seaside locale, we scattered shells and sand dollars on the table and placed sea grass in vases filled with sand and smooth stones; if you're not at the beach, other greenery will do.

Menu

Lobster, Potato & Green Bean Salad
with Pesto Vinaigrette

—

Maple Syrup & Mustard-glazed
Poussins

Fresh Corn & Polenta Cakes

Honey-baked Tomatoes
with Crusty Topping

Spiced Peaches

—

Warm Blueberry Shortcakes

Inspired by New England cuisine, our al fresco lunch features summertime favorites such as lobster, sweet corn, maple syrup and fresh blueberries. All the recipes are easily prepared, since much of the work may be done in advance and the last-minute cooking is limited primarily to the main course. With a few substitutions, these recipes can be made at any time of year.

To mark this unique occasion, you might want to bake an extra batch of dessert shortcakes and package them in paper bags tied with raffia or twine for guests to take home. Try knotting shells onto the ties as a reminder of the seaside theme.

WINE RECOMMENDATIONS

With the lobster salad, sip a rich white with herbal accents, ample body and acidity: a Sauvignon Blanc or a northern Italian white wine. With the main course, try a spicy white Riesling or an off-dry blush wine. For dessert, a chilled ruby port or a black Muscat.

Package extra shortcake biscuits in decorated bags as gifts for guests. Left, trophy cups or an assortment of other unique containers make ideal vases for displaying sea grass. Fill with sand and smooth stones to weight them down in case of sudden gusts.

PREPARATION LIST

- 1 week ahead of time, prepare the spiced peaches.

- The night before, cook and refrigerate the lobsters in their shells. Coat the poussins; cook and refrigerate the polenta to be cut into triangles the next day.

- The morning of the party, bake the shortcake biscuits, rewarm in the oven before serving.

- One hour ahead, cook the potatoes and green beans for the salad.

EACH RECIPE YIELDS 6 SERVINGS

A tray holds small glasses of chilled ruby port to accompany the shortcakes for dessert.

LOBSTER, POTATO & GREEN BEAN SALAD WITH PESTO VINAIGRETTE

SERVES 6

A relative of salade niçoise, this extravagant first course is also delicious made with shrimp or fresh tuna. Try the dressing on grilled fish or chicken.

salt
3 live Atlantic (Maine) lobsters, 1–1¼ lb (500–625 g) each
12–18 small red new potatoes (creamers) or yellow Finnish potatoes, about 2 lb (1 kg) total
1½ lb (750 g) green beans, trimmed and cut into 2-inch (5-cm) lengths
1 cup (1½ oz/45 g) tightly packed fresh basil leaves
1 teaspoon minced garlic
2 tablespoons toasted pine nuts or walnuts (see glossary)
about ¾ cup (6 fl oz/180 ml) olive oil
¼ cup (2 fl oz/60 ml) red wine vinegar
freshly ground pepper
butter lettuce
cherry tomatoes

*B*ring a very large pot of salted water to a boil. Drop in the lobsters and cook, covered, for 10 minutes. Remove the lobsters from the pot and drop them into a sinkful of ice water. (If desired, refrigerate the lobsters overnight.) Cut each lobster in half lengthwise and remove the meat from the body and claws as directed on page 188; discard the shells. Cut the meat into bite-sized pieces, place in a bowl, cover and refrigerate until serving.

❧ Place the potatoes in a saucepan, cover them with cold water and add salt. Bring to a boil, then reduce heat and simmer, uncovered, until the potatoes are cooked through but still firm, about 10–20 minutes. Drain and refrigerate to stop further cooking.

❧ Bring a large pot of salted water to a boil. Drop in the green beans and cook until tender-crisp, about 2–4 minutes. Drain the beans and plunge them into ice water. Drain, pat dry and set aside.

❧ Combine the basil leaves, garlic and nuts in a food processor or blender. Pulse to combine. Add about ½ cup (4 fl oz/125 ml) of the olive oil and process to a coarse purée. Transfer the pesto to a bowl and stir in the vinegar and enough of the remaining oil to make a spoonable vinaigrette. Season with salt and pepper.

❧ To serve, cut the potatoes into ¼-inch (6-mm) slices. In a large bowl, toss the potatoes and green beans with half the vinaigrette. Divide among 6 salad plates lined with lettuce leaves; top with lobster pieces and drizzle with the remaining vinaigrette. Garnish with cherry tomatoes.

*L*arge and small seashells and brightly colored coral accent the table.

*L*obster, Potato & Green Bean Salad with Pesto Vinaigrette

MAPLE SYRUP— & MUSTARD-GLAZED POUSSINS

SERVES 6

Take care not to overcook these little chickens: When done, their flesh remains slightly pink. Another time, try quail.

6 poussins or Cornish hens, about 1 lb (500 g) each, or 12 quail
2 teaspoons dry mustard
½ teaspoon ground cinnamon
2 tablespoons cider vinegar
⅔ cup (5 fl oz/160 ml) maple syrup
3 tablespoons prepared Dijon mustard
2 tablespoons soy sauce
salt and freshly ground pepper to taste
oil for brushing

*B*utterfly the poussins or Cornish hens: Insert a sharp knife through the neck cavity of each bird and carefully cut down one side of the backbone. Cut along the other side of the backbone to remove it from the body. Press on the breastbone of each bird to flatten it. (You may leave the quail whole.)
ஃ In a bowl, combine the dry mustard, cinnamon and vinegar and mix into a paste. Add the maple syrup, prepared mustard and soy sauce and adjust the seasoning; it should be spicy but sweet. Spread half of this mixture evenly over the birds, cover and let sit at room temperature for 1 hour or refrigerate for up to 8 hours. Reserve the remaining half of the paste for basting.
ஃ Preheat a broiler (griller). Or, prepare a fire in a grill; position the oiled grill rack 4–6 inches (10–15 cm) above the fire. Sprinkle the birds with salt and pepper and brush with a little oil. Broil the poussins or hens, or grill them over medium-hot coals, flesh-side down for 5 minutes, then brush with the glaze, turn and cook for 5 minutes longer. (Cook quail for 3–4 minutes on each side.)

FRESH CORN & POLENTA CAKES

SERVES 6

Look for polenta in a well-stocked food shop or an Italian grocer. When cooked and cooled, it can be cut into any shape.

4 ears corn or 3 cups (1¼ lb/625 g) thawed frozen corn kernels
1½ cups (9 oz/280 g) polenta or coarse yellow cornmeal
6 cups (48 fl oz/1.5 l) cold water or more as needed
salt and freshly ground pepper to taste
about ½ cup (4 fl oz/125 ml) olive oil or vegetable oil
minced fresh chives

*I*f using ears of corn, cut the kernels off the ears with a large knife. Drop the corn kernels into boiling salted water and cook for 1–2 minutes. Drain the corn and rinse in cold water. Dry very well on paper towels.
ஃ Combine the polenta or cornmeal and cold water in a large saucepan. Cook over low heat, stirring often, until thick and no longer grainy on the tongue, 20–30 minutes. Add more water gradually if the polenta is thick but still grainy. When the polenta is done, stir in the corn kernels. Season with salt and pepper and spread in an even layer in an oiled baking sheet with sides; the polenta should be about ¾ inch (2 cm) thick. Cover with plastic wrap and refrigerate until firm.
ஃ To serve, cut the polenta into circles, triangles or rectangles. Heat the oil in a frying pan to a depth of ¼ inch (6 mm) and sauté the polenta pieces until pale gold on both sides, about 5 minutes total. Transfer to plates and sprinkle with chives.

HONEY-BAKED TOMATOES WITH CRUSTY TOPPING

SERVES 6

Basting with honey highlights the natural sweetness of these baked tomatoes. If desired, place each tomato on a plate with a handful of fresh watercress or arugula sprigs for a refreshingly bitter contrast.

1½ cups (3 oz/90 g) fresh bread crumbs
½ cup (4 fl oz/125 ml) olive oil
1 teaspoon salt
½ teaspoon freshly ground pepper
6 tablespoons (4 oz/125 g) honey
pinch of ground nutmeg
6 ripe tomatoes

*P*reheat an oven to 350°F (180°C). Spread the bread crumbs on a baking sheet, toss with 6 tablespoons (3 fl oz/90 ml) of the oil and sprinkle with ½ teaspoon of the salt and the pepper. Bake, stirring often, until golden and slightly crunchy but not hard, about 20 minutes. Set aside, leaving the oven on.
ஃ In a small saucepan over low heat, warm the honey, remaining 2 tablespoons of oil and the nutmeg.
ஃ Cut a slice off the stem end of each tomato. Place the tomatoes in a baking dish. Sprinkle with the remaining ½ teaspoon salt, brush the top of each tomato with a little of the honey mixture and top each tomato with some of the bread crumbs, pressing them into the tomato. Bake the tomatoes until soft and lightly browned on top, basting with the honey mixture several times, about 15–20 minutes.

Maple Syrup– & Mustard-glazed Poussins;
Fresh Corn & Polenta Cakes;
Honey-baked Tomatoes with Crusty Topping

SPICED PEACHES

MAKES 12 PEACHES

A classic American conserve, these keep for up to a month in the refrigerator or up to a year when canned. Serve them with the main course, cut in half, pitted and garnished with watercress.

1½ cups (12 fl oz/375 ml) cider vinegar
1½ cups (12 fl oz/375 ml) water
2 cups (1 lb/500 g) sugar
3 sticks cinnamon
10–12 whole cloves
1 teaspoon black peppercorns
2 strips lemon zest
12 firm ripe peaches

Combine the vinegar, water, sugar, cinnamon, cloves, peppercorns and lemon zest in a large, deep enameled or stainless-steel saucepan. Bring to a boil and stir until the sugar dissolves. Reduce the heat and simmer the syrup for 10 minutes.

❧ Meanwhile, drop a few peaches at a time into a large pot of boiling water for 1–2 minutes to loosen the skin. Lift out with a slotted spoon, let cool briefly, then peel. Add the peaches to the hot syrup and poach for 2 minutes, then remove them with a slotted spoon and place in 2 sterilized 4-cup (32-fl oz/1-l) canning jars. Spoon the syrup over the peaches to within ½ inch (12 mm) of the top and seal the jars. Process in a hot-water bath for 25–30 minutes (see Canning, page 186), or store in the refrigerator for up to 1 month.

Spiced Peaches

Cluster sea treasures in a half shell.

WARM BLUEBERRY SHORTCAKES

SERVES 6

Classic cream biscuits accompany this variation on strawberry shortcake.

FOR THE SHORTCAKES:

1¾ cups (9 oz/280 g) all-purpose
   (plain) flour
½ teaspoon salt
1 tablespoon baking powder
2 teaspoons sugar
6 tablespoons (3 oz/90 g) unsalted
   butter or vegetable shortening
   (vegetable lard), chilled
1 cup (8 fl oz/250 ml) milk or heavy
   (double) cream
grated zest of 1 orange or 2 lemons
about 3 tablespoons unsalted butter,
   melted, or heavy (double) cream

FOR THE BLUEBERRY COMPOTE:

6 cups (1½ lb/750 g) fresh or thawed
   frozen whole blueberries
2 tablespoons fresh lemon juice
1 teaspoon ground cinnamon
1½ cups (12 oz/375 g) sugar
grated zest of 1 lemon or 1 orange

FOR THE MAPLE WHIPPED CREAM:

1 cup (8 fl oz/250 ml) heavy
   (double) cream
2 tablespoons maple syrup
¼ teaspoon vanilla extract (essence)

*P*reheat an oven to 450°F (230°C). To make the shortcakes, combine the flour, salt, baking powder and sugar in a medium bowl. Cut the butter or shortening into bits, then blend into the flour mixture with a pastry cutter or 2 knives until the mixture resembles cornmeal. Make a well in the center and add the milk or cream and zest. Stir quickly until the dough comes free from the sides of the bowl, about 1 minute. Turn the dough out onto a lightly floured board and knead gently and quickly, turning it about 12 times, or until the dough is no longer sticky. Pat into a ½-inch-thick (12-mm) square.

❧ Dipping a 2¼-inch (5.5-cm) cutter into flour each time, cut the dough into 12 round or square biscuits. Place on an ungreased baking sheet, brush the tops with the melted butter or the cream and bake on the middle rack of the oven until pale gold, 12–15 minutes.

❧ Meanwhile, to make the compote, combine 4 cups (1 lb/500 g) of the blueberries with the lemon juice, cinnamon, sugar and zest in a heavy saucepan over moderate heat. Simmer until thickened and hot, about 5 minutes. Stir in the remaining blueberries and set aside.

❧ To make the maple whipped cream, in a bowl beat the cream, maple syrup and vanilla until it forms soft peaks.

❧ To serve, split the warm biscuits in half crosswise. Place 2 bottoms on each of 6 individual plates. Spoon half of the blueberry compote on the biscuits, add a dollop of whipped cream and a little more compote to each, then top with the remaining biscuit halves. Spoon on remaining compote and serve at once.

Warm Blueberry Shortcakes

POOLSIDE FIESTA

Traditional summer holidays and other special events at the height of the season call for high-spirited entertaining. To beat the heat, plan the party for late in the day, when evening breezes begin to stir. A deck beside a swimming pool is a perfect spot, but any patio, large balcony, airy dining room or picnic area in the countryside will do.

The Latin tastes of this menu inspired us to assemble the hottest-colored accessories we could find: heavy, peasant-style pottery and coarse linens in reds, yellows, greens and blues. We chose flowers from the same palette, added bouquets of fresh chili peppers and arranged them in brightly colored Latin American food tins (found in ethnic markets). The tables were draped with woven Mexican rugs and chairs of all kinds were pressed into use for seating around large outdoor dining tables set end to end.

Menu

Caipirinha Cocktail & Pineapple Batida

Latin American Fish Brochettes with
Peanut-Tomato Salsa

———

Grilled Steaks with Chimichurri Sauce

Tomatoes with Avocado Salsa

Latin American Potato Salad

Grilled Peppered Bananas with Bacon

Grilled Corn on the Cob with
Chili-Lime Butter

———

Caipirinha (Rum & Lime Cream) Pie

A poolside fiesta is the natural setting for a menu of easily prepared, quickly grilled foods with enough variety to please everyone. The recipes here take their inspiration from *churrascos*, the traditional outdoor barbecues of Argentina and Brazil. These spicy, but not-too-hot dishes, complemented by icy rum cocktails, beer or wine, are perfect for any summer party.

To make inexpensive table decorations, try scoring the peels of lemons, limes and oranges in decorative patterns with a citrus zester; tie napkins with bright ribbons knotted around the stems of fresh chilies. Place tropical fruits, such as papayas and pineapples, down the center of the table and use whole bell peppers, their stems cut out, as colorful holders for votive candles to light the table as evening falls.

WINE RECOMMENDATIONS

Though some guests may continue to sip their cocktails with the first course, offer a light red wine such as a young Beaujolais or a Pinot Noir. With the steaks, pour a bold, country-style red: American Zinfandel or Chilean Cabernet Sauvignon. Beer, of course, is also good throughout the meal, and Asti Spumante or Muscat would be a refreshing choice to serve with dessert.

Lined with heavy-duty plastic bags and filled with ice, an old toy pedal car or a wagon makes a whimsical vehicle for chilling beer, wine or other beverages. Left, empty colorful food tins are used to display pepper bouquets.

PREPARATION LIST

• Up to 8 hours ahead, make the pie, cover and refrigerate; marinate the steaks.

• Up to 5 hours ahead, make the peanut-tomato salsa for the fish and the chimichurri sauce for the meat.

• Up to 3 hours before, butter, wrap and refrigerate the corn; mix and refrigerate the potato salad.

• Two hours ahead, make the avocado salsa.

• One hour before, preheat the grill; wrap the bananas in bacon; marinate the fish.

EACH FOOD RECIPE YIELDS 12 SERVINGS. MAKE THE DRINKS IN BATCHES OF 2, AS NOT EVERYONE WILL BE CONSUMING HARD LIQUOR.

Spice up your table with a chili pepper and a ribbon knotted around each napkin.

CAIPIRINHA COCKTAIL

MAKES 2 DRINKS

A national drink of Brazil, this lime-and-rum cocktail packs a wallop and is great with spicy foods. Serve with chunks of lime in each glass.

1 juicy lime, cut into 6 pieces
2 heaping teaspoons confectioners'
 (icing) or superfine (caster) sugar
2 shot glasses (3 fl oz/90 ml) cachaça
 (Brazilian sugarcane rum) or light rum
2 cups (10 oz/315 g) ice cubes

Place the lime in a beverage shaker and press down hard on it with a pestle or a wooden spoon to mash the pulp and release the juice. Add the rest of the ingredients and shake well. Pour the liquid, lime, ice and all into tall glasses.

PINEAPPLE BATIDA

MAKES 2 DRINKS

Batida means "beaten" in Portuguese—an apt description for this frothy tropical punch.

⅓ cup (3 fl oz/90 ml) pineapple juice
4 teaspoons superfine (caster) sugar
2 tablespoons fresh lemon juice
2 shot glasses (3 fl oz/90 ml) cachaça
 (Brazilian sugarcane rum) or light rum
2 cups (10 oz/315 g) ice cubes

Combine all of the ingredients in a shaker and shake well. Pour the liquid and ice cubes into tall glasses.

LATIN AMERICAN FISH BROCHETTES WITH PEANUT-TOMATO SALSA

SERVES 12

Don't marinate these appetizers more than an hour, or the citrus juices will "cook" the fish like a ceviche. Use swordfish, halibut, mahi-mahi or seabass.

FOR THE SALSA:

½ cup (2½ oz/75 g) roasted peanuts
 (salted or unsalted), coarsely chopped
2 cups (12 oz/375 g) finely chopped
 peeled, seeded tomatoes
½ cup (2½ oz/75 g) minced onions
½ cup (4 fl oz/125 ml) fresh lemon juice
2 cloves garlic, minced
3 jalapeño (hot green) chili peppers,
 seeded and minced
1–2 tablespoons finely grated fresh
 ginger or to taste
2 tablespoons chopped cilantro
 (fresh coriander)
½ cup (4 fl oz/125 ml) olive oil

FOR THE BROCHETTES:

3 lb (1.5 kg) firm white-fleshed fish or
 48 large shrimp (prawns)
8 cloves garlic, minced
3–4 jalapeño (hot green) chili peppers,
 seeded and minced, or ½ teaspoon
 or more cayenne pepper
2 tablespoons ground cumin
2 tablespoons ground coriander
½ cup (4 fl oz/125 ml) fresh lemon or
 lime juice or red wine vinegar
½ cup (4 fl oz/125 ml) olive oil
salt and freshly ground pepper to taste

To make the salsa, combine all of the ingredients in a medium bowl; cover and set aside for up to 5 hours.
❧ To prepare the brochettes, cut the fish into 1-inch (2.5-cm) cubes or, if you are using shrimp, shell and devein them. In a small bowl, mix the garlic,

jalapeños, cumin and coriander into a paste with the lemon juice (or lime juice or vinegar). Whisk in the oil. Place the fish or shrimp in a glass or plastic container, pour the marinade over and toss. Cover and marinate in the refrigerator for 30–60 minutes, stirring once or twice.
❧ Meanwhile, prepare a fire in a grill. Position the oiled grill rack 4–6 inches (10–15 cm) above the fire. Or, preheat a broiler (griller).
❧ Remove the fish or shrimp from the marinade and thread on 12 skewers. Sprinkle with salt and pepper. Grill over hot coals or broil until the fish turns opaque in the center or until the shrimp are pink, about 2 minutes on each side. Serve with the salsa.

For a natural decoration, use a zesting tool to score folk-art-style designs on citrus fruits.

Caipirinha Cocktail; Pineapple Batida; Latin American Fish Brochettes with Peanut-Tomato Salsa

GRILLED STEAKS WITH CHIMICHURRI SAUCE

SERVES 12

Chimichurri, a traditional Argentine table sauce for grilled meat, is also excellent on grilled chicken or seafood.

FOR THE CHIMICHURRI SAUCE:

1 cup (8 fl oz/250 ml) olive oil
½ cup (4 fl oz/125 ml) red
    wine vinegar
½ cup (4 fl oz/125 ml) fresh
    orange juice
grated zest of 1 orange
1 cup (5 oz/155 g) minced onions
1 tablespoon minced garlic
½ cup (¾ oz/20 g) minced
    fresh parsley
1 tablespoon dried oregano
1 teaspoon cayenne pepper

FOR THE STEAKS:

3 large onions, finely chopped
8 cloves garlic, minced
3 tablespoons chili powder
2 tablespoons ground cumin
2 tablespoons freshly ground pepper
2 tablespoons dried oregano
1 cup (8 fl oz/250 ml) fresh
    lemon juice
salt to taste
4 large flank steaks, about 1½ lb
    (750 g) each

To make the chimichurri sauce, combine all the ingredients in a medium bowl; cover and set aside for up to 5 hours. Makes about 2½ cups (20 fl oz/625 ml).

Grilled Steaks with Chimichurri Sauce;
Latin American Potato Salad;
Tomatoes with Avocado Salsa

To prepare the steaks, place the onions, garlic, chili powder, cumin, pepper, oregano and lemon juice in a blender or food processor and purée; season with salt. Place the steaks in a large glass or plastic container and pour the purée over the meat. Cover and marinate for 2 hours at room temperature or refrigerate overnight.

Prepare a fire in a grill. Position the oiled grill rack 4–6 inches (10–15 cm) above the fire.

When the coals are hot, grill the steaks, turning once, until cooked to your liking, about 3 minutes on each side for rare and 4 minutes on each side for medium rare. Slice the steaks across the grain and serve with the sauce.

TOMATOES WITH AVOCADO SALSA

SERVES 12

This all-purpose salsa is also good with grilled meat, poultry or fish, or spooned inside quesadillas (recipe on page 169).

3 avocados
8 plum tomatoes or 4 regular tomatoes, peeled, seeded and diced
1 tablespoon minced seeded jalapeño (hot green) chili pepper
¼ cup (2 oz/60 g) minced green bell pepper (capsicum)
¼ cup (2 fl oz/60 ml) fresh lemon juice
2 tablespoons red wine vinegar
½ cup (4 fl oz/125 ml) olive oil
2 tablespoons chopped cilantro (fresh coriander)
salt and freshly ground pepper to taste
6 large, firm ripe beefsteak tomatoes

Cut the avocados in half, remove the pits and scoop from the shell with a large spoon. Finely dice the avocados.

In a bowl, combine the avocados, diced tomatoes, jalapeño, bell pepper, lemon juice, vinegar, oil and cilantro. Season with salt and pepper and refrigerate for up to 2 hours.

Slice the beefsteak tomatoes and arrange the slices on a platter or individual plates; spoon the avocado salsa over the slices.

LATIN AMERICAN POTATO SALAD

SERVES 12

Potatoes originated in Peru, where this robust salad finds its inspiration. The tangy feta resembles Peruvian queso fresco.

36 small red or white new potatoes (depending on size), about 4 lb (2 kg)
1 cup (5 oz/155 g) minced red (Spanish) onions
1 cup (3 oz/90 g) minced green (spring) onions
3 red or green bell peppers (capsicums), stemmed, seeded, deribbed and diced
6 minced seeded jalapeño (hot green) chili peppers
4 cloves garlic, minced
8 anchovy fillets, minced fine, about 1 tablespoon
¾ cup (6 fl oz/185 ml) red wine vinegar
1 cup (8 fl oz/250 ml) olive oil
2 cups (10 oz/315 g) coarsely crumbled feta cheese
6 hard-cooked eggs, cut into quarters
¼ cup (⅜ oz/10 g) minced cilantro (fresh coriander)
black olives, such as Kalamata or niçoise, for garnish

Place the potatoes in a large saucepan and cover them with cold salted water. Bring to a boil, then reduce heat and simmer, uncovered, until they are

cooked through but still firm, about 12–18 minutes, depending on the size of the potatoes. Drain immediately and refrigerate to stop further cooking.

When the potatoes are cool, cut them into halves or quarters. Combine the potatoes, onions and bell peppers in a large bowl and set aside. Combine the jalapeños, garlic and anchovies in a medium bowl or large mortar. Using the back of a large spoon or a pestle, mash this mixture to a paste with some of the vinegar. Add the rest of the vinegar, then whisk in the olive oil. Toss the potatoes, peppers and onions with this vinaigrette. Gently fold in the feta cheese and hard-cooked eggs. Cover and refrigerate for up to 3 hours. Serve garnished with the minced cilantro and olives.

Place tropical fruits directly on the table for a carefree centerpiece.

GRILLED PEPPERED BANANAS WITH BACON

SERVES 12

Warm and sweet, this side dish soothes the palate between bites of spicy food. Try wrapping and grilling fresh pineapple spears, too. If using bamboo skewers, be sure to soak them in warm water for at least 20 minutes first.

6 bananas
freshly ground pepper to taste
12 strips bacon

Prepare a fire in a grill. Position the oiled grill rack 4–6 inches (10–15 cm) above the fire.

❧ Peel the bananas and cut them in half crosswise. Sprinkle each half with pepper and wrap in a piece of bacon. Thread 1 banana half on each of 12 skewers. When the coals are medium-hot, place the bananas on the grill and cook, turning as needed, until the bacon is crisp and the bananas are lightly browned, about 5 minutes.

GRILLED CORN ON THE COB WITH CHILI-LIME BUTTER

SERVES 12

The hint of citrus and chili highlights the corn's natural sweetness. Serve with extra lime wedges to squeeze over the corn.

12 ears corn
¾ cup (6 oz/180 g) unsalted butter at room temperature
2 tablespoons chili powder
½ teaspoon cayenne pepper
1 teaspoon paprika
grated zest of 2 limes
¼ cup (2 fl oz/60 ml) fresh lime juice

Remove the husks from the corn. In a bowl, mix the butter, chili powder, cayenne, paprika, lime zest and juice. Spread 1 tablespoon of butter on each ear of corn, then wrap each ear in a large piece of aluminum foil. Refrigerate for up to 3 hours.

❧ Prepare a fire in a grill. Position the oiled grill rack 4–6 inches (10–15 cm) above the fire. When the coals are hot, place the corn on the grill and cook, turning once or twice with tongs, for 10 minutes. Remove the foil before serving.

CAIPIRINHA (RUM & LIME CREAM) PIE

MAKES TWO 9-INCH (23-CM) PIES

This tangy-creamy dessert gets its name from the national Brazilian cocktail.

Basic pie pastry for a double-crust pie shell (recipe on page 177)
2 tablespoons (2 envelopes) unflavored gelatin dissolved in 1 cup (8 fl oz/250 ml) fresh lime juice
1 cup (8 fl oz/250 ml) dark rum
12 egg yolks
2 cups (1 lb/500 g) sugar
grated zest of 4 limes
4 cups (32 fl oz/1 l) heavy (double) cream
1½ cups (5 oz/155 g) toasted flaked coconut (see glossary)

Divide the pastry in half. Roll out both halves and use to line two 9-inch (23-cm) pie pans; flute the rims. Set aside in the freezer for 30 minutes or overnight. Fully bake the pie shells as directed on page 177. Cool completely before filling.

❧ Warm the dissolved gelatin and rum in a small saucepan. In a large bowl, beat the egg yolks, gradually adding the sugar, until the mixture is very thick and pale. Fold the gelatin mixture and zest into the yolks. Beat the cream until stiff and fold it into the yolks. Chill the filling until it begins to set, about 30 minutes.

❧ Divide the filling equally between the cooked pie shells, then refrigerate until set completely, about 1½ hours. Top each pie with toasted coconut and serve.

Grilled Peppered Bananas with Bacon, Grilled Corn on the Cob with Chili-Lime Butter (above); Caipirinha (Rum & Lime Cream) Pie (at right)

INDIAN SUMMER BRUNCH

There is a special poignancy to those few weeks in autumn when summer's warmth comes rushing back, calling us outdoors once again. This is an ideal time of year for casual weekend brunches to celebrate birthdays or anniversaries, sports events, or a visit from out-of-town guests.

We set our brunch on a deck framed by trees, but a terrace, a garden or a breakfast nook is fine. Indian summer suggested a color scheme of deep reds, russets and warm golds for table decorations; bright sunflowers and bowls of small lady apples brought this to life. The comforting nature of the recipes inspired the use of homespun touches such as a patchwork quilt for a table-cloth, milk served in an old-fashioned dairy bottle and napkins knotted around miniature rolling pins. The arrival of a friend's puppy happily completed the scene.

Menu

North African Orange Salad

—

Baked Eggs, Merguez Sausage,
Peppers & Tomatoes

Toast

Herbed Lemon Marmalade

—

Moroccan Pancakes with
Almond Cream

To echo the vibrant contrasts of this time of year, this menu combines familiar breakfast dishes with exotic North African flavors. Much of the preparation can be done in advance, allowing you to enjoy the morning along with your guests. The choice of dishes allows a leisurely pace of eating.

For the easiest service, start the meal with individual plates of salad on the table along with baskets of toast and jars of marmalade. The eggs can be served directly from the baking dish (nestled in a basket for comfortable handling), followed by the pancakes. Offer a range of hot and cold beverages, including pitchers of sparkling-wine-and-orange-juice mimosas, pots of coffee flavored with cinnamon or cardamom and tea with cinnamon or mint.

WINE RECOMMENDATIONS

Coffee, tea or mimosas may be sipped throughout the meal. But, if you like, with the salad you could also pour a light Riesling or an Italian Moscato d'Asti. That wine could be continued with the eggs, or you could switch to a brut Champagne or sparkling wine with a good amount of Chardonnay in the blend.

For the guests, casually tie cotton napkins around a simple host or hostess gift such as a toy rolling pin. Left, a bowl of small apples displayed on the dining table captures the hues of Indian summer.

PREPARATION LIST

• Two weeks before the brunch, make the marmalade (or use purchased marmalade).

• The night before, prepare and refrigerate the almond cream; make and refrigerate the sausage and pepper mixtures for the eggs.

• About 30 minutes before serving the salad, prepare the pancake batter.

• After serving the eggs, cook and top the pancakes.

EACH RECIPE YIELDS 6 SERVINGS

In place of quiet music on the stereo, let the summer breeze provide the party's score, gently ringing bells or chimes suspended from a nearby tree.

NORTH AFRICAN ORANGE SALAD

SERVES 6

Sweet and savory, this orange and olive salad is a nice foil to the spicy egg dish that follows. In winter, try making it with blood oranges.

6 regular oranges or blood oranges
18 Moroccan olives or cured black olives
3 bunches watercress
½ teaspoon ground cinnamon
2 tablespoons confectioners' (icing) sugar
¼ cup (2 fl oz/60 ml) olive oil
3 tablespoons fresh lemon juice
pinch of salt
½ teaspoon ground cumin

Grate the zest of 1 of the oranges and set aside. Remove the peel and pith of all the oranges and cut between the membranes to release all the segments. Remove all seeds. If the oranges are small, simply slice the oranges into rounds and remove the seeds.

❧ Cut the olives in half and remove the pits, or leave them whole. Trim the tough stems from the watercress.

❧ Combine the cinnamon and confectioners' sugar in a shaker, or use a small wire sieve. In a large bowl, combine the oil, lemon juice, salt, cumin and grated zest. Add the watercress and olives and toss well; divide among 6 plates. Top with the orange slices or segments. Sprinkle the oranges with the cinnamon sugar.

North African Orange Salad

BAKED EGGS, MERGUEZ SAUSAGE, PEPPERS & TOMATOES

SERVES 6

Easily assembled, this baked egg dish, known in Tunisia as chakchouka, *features North African–style fresh sausage patties and a pepper-tomato medley.*

FOR THE MERGUEZ:

1 lb (500 g) ground lamb or beef, not too lean
2 cloves garlic, minced
½ teaspoon ground cinnamon
¼–½ teaspoon cayenne pepper, or to taste
1 teaspoon ground cumin
1 tablespoon sweet Hungarian paprika
1 teaspoon ground coriander
1½ teaspoons salt
½ teaspoon freshly ground pepper
2 tablespoons water

FOR THE SAUCE:

3 tablespoons olive oil
2 onions, coarsely chopped
2 cloves garlic, minced
3 large green or red bell peppers (capsicums), stemmed, seeded, deribbed and coarsely chopped
4 large tomatoes, peeled, seeded and chopped
¼ cup (⅜ oz/10 g) chopped cilantro (fresh coriander) and/or parsley
salt and freshly ground pepper to taste

FOR ASSEMBLY:

1 tablespoon olive oil
merguez patties, above
sauce, above
12 eggs

To make the merguez, combine the lamb, garlic, cinnamon, cayenne, cumin, paprika, coriander, salt, pepper and water in a food processor. Pulse to

Baked Eggs, Merguez Sausage, Peppers & Tomatoes; Herbed Lemon Marmalade (page 78)

combine. Form into 12 oval patties; cover and refrigerate for up to 8 hours.
ঌ To make the sauce, heat the oil in a large sauté pan. Add the onions and cook over moderate heat until soft, about 10 minutes. Add the garlic and peppers and cook until soft, about 5 minutes. Then add the tomatoes and cook until the tomatoes have melted down, about 10

minutes longer. Stir in the cilantro and/or parsley and season with salt and pepper. Cover and refrigerate for up to 8 hours.
ঌ To assemble, preheat an oven to 400°F (200°C). Heat the oil in a heavy frying pan over high heat. Brown the merguez patties on both sides. Remove from the skillet and drain on paper towels. Spoon the sauce into a large

baking dish. Arrange the merguez patties around the perimeter, then break the eggs into the center. Or, divide the sauce among 6 small gratin dishes, place 2 merguez patties in each gratin dish, then break 2 eggs into each one. Bake until the whites are set but the yolks are still soft, about 20 minutes for the large dish, about 8–10 minutes for individual gratins.

HERBED LEMON MARMALADE

MAKES 8 CUPS (64 OZ/2 KG)

Fresh mint and mint tea combine with lemon verbena and orange flower water to perfume this preserve. Let the marmalade rest for 2 weeks before serving.

4 lb (2 kg) large, juicy lemons, about 10–12

10 cups (2½ qt/2.5 l) cold water

4 mint tea bags

8 cups (4 lb/2 kg) sugar

3 tablespoons orange flower water, optional

32 whole mint leaves

16 lemon verbena leaves, optional

Wash and dry the lemons. Remove the zest with a vegetable peeler, being careful not to remove any pith; cut zest into very thin strips and place in a saucepan, cover with about 1 cup (8 fl oz/250 ml) of the water and bring to a boil. Cook for 2 minutes, then discard the water. Cover with 1 more cup (8 fl oz/250 ml) of the water and soak the zest overnight.

è Cut the peeled lemons in half crosswise and slice as thinly as possible. Remove the seeds. Put the sliced lemons in a large, heavy enameled or stainless-steel pot. Cover with the remaining 8 cups (64 fl oz/2 l) water and let soak overnight.

è The next day, bring the lemons to a boil with the mint tea bags and simmer, uncovered, for 15 minutes. Let sit for 3 hours, then remove and discard the tea bags. Add the soaked zest and sugar and bring to a boil. Simmer, uncovered, until a small spoonful of the mixture gels slightly on a chilled plate, about 35 minutes. Stir in the optional orange flower water. Place 2 mint leaves and

1 optional lemon verbena leaf in the bottom of each of 8 hot sterilized 1-cup (8-fl oz/250-ml) canning jars. Pour in the marmalade, leaving ½ inch (12 mm) of head space, top with the remaining leaves, then seal the jars. Process in a hot-water bath for 10 minutes (see Canning, page 186), or store in the refrigerator for up to 3 months. *(Pictured on previous page.)*

MOROCCAN PANCAKES WITH ALMOND CREAM

SERVES 6

These yeast-leavened pancakes are more substantial than most Western pancakes.

FOR THE ALMOND CREAM:

4 cups (32 fl oz/1 l) milk

¾ cup (3 oz/90 g) ground toasted almonds (see glossary)

¾ cup (6 oz/185 g) sugar

¼ cup (1 oz/30 g) cornstarch (cornflour)

4 egg yolks

1 teaspoon vanilla extract (essence)

½ teaspoon almond extract (essence)

2 tablespoons orange flower water

FOR THE PANCAKES:

1 tablespoon active dry yeast

1 teaspoon sugar

¼ cup (2 fl oz/60 ml) warm (110°F/43°C) water

1½ cups (7½ oz/235 g) all-purpose (plain) flour

¼ teaspoon salt

¼ teaspoon ground cinnamon

1 egg

1¼ cups (10 fl oz/300 ml) milk

TO COOK AND SERVE:

oil for cooking

6 small bananas

¾ cup (3 oz/90 g) toasted whole or slivered almonds (see glossary)

julienne strips of orange zest, optional

To prepare the almond cream, combine the milk, the almonds and half of the sugar in a medium saucepan. Place over moderate heat and bring to scalding. Remove from heat, cover the pan and let steep for 30 minutes. Strain, pressing down on the almonds with the back of a spoon to release the most flavor possible. Reheat the milk. In a small bowl, combine the cornstarch, remaining sugar and egg yolks; beat in a small amount of the warm milk. Pour this mixture back into the pan and cook, stirring, over moderate heat until the mixture thickens and boils for 1–2 minutes. Remove from the heat and stir in the extracts and the orange flower water. Let cool, then cover and refrigerate for up to 8 hours.

è To make the pancakes, combine the yeast, sugar and warm water in a small bowl. Set aside in a warm place until foamy, about 10 minutes. Sift the flour, salt and cinnamon together into a medium bowl. Make a well in the center and add the yeast mixture. In a small bowl, beat together the egg and milk. Stir gradually into the flour and yeast mixture until a smooth batter is formed. Cover the bowl and let the mixture rise in a warm place for 1 hour.

è Brush a griddle with oil, heat until very hot, then lower the heat to moderate. Drop heaping tablespoonfuls of batter on the griddle. Cook until bubbles appear. Turn the pancakes over and cook until golden brown, about 1 minute longer. Transfer to baking sheets, but do not stack. Keep warm in a low oven.

è Slice the bananas and fold them into the almond cream. Spoon over the warm pancakes and top with the toasted almonds and, if desired, the orange zest. Serve at once.

Moroccan Pancakes with Almond Cream

HARVEST LUNCH

In vineyards and on farms everywhere, family, friends and co-workers stop harvesting at midday to share a simple feast that highlights nature's bounty. Here, we chose a vineyard location, but you don't need to live or work in the countryside to enjoy this autumnal celebration. Whether you set your table beneath trees, on a patio or near a sunny window, what matters is an abundance of seasonal food and a spirit of fellowship.

We aimed to capture the feel of the harvest by using a rustic, weather-beaten table, setting it with ceramic dishes and simple cutlery. For the centerpiece, we gathered wildflowers from a nearby garden; any mixed seasonal blooms from a flower vendor do just as well. Fresh fruit or grape clusters, bunches of autumn leaves and vine trimmings are also fitting tokens of the harvest to add to your decorations.

Menu

Grilled Peppered Figs with
Grilled Goat Cheese in Grape Leaves

Walnut Focaccia

———

Butterflied Leg of Lamb in
Middle Eastern Yogurt Marinade

Spiced Apricot Chutney

Grilled Eggplant with
Sweet Cherry Tomato Sauce

Lentil Salad

———

Blue Plum Tart

The menu that follows features seasonal fare that's abundant, yet simple to prepare. While the ingredients are readily available in food stores, the best fruits and vegetables—especially figs and blue plums—are usually found at your local farmer's market. And be sure to take advantage of this occasion to offer one or more of your favorite vintage or varietal wines.

This menu doesn't have to be limited by the seasons, however. With the substitutions suggested in the recipe introductions, you'll find that these dishes can be reliable standbys at lunches and dinners throughout the year.

WINE RECOMMENDATIONS

Celebrate the harvest with a choice of flavorful young white and red wines. Choose a white with generous flavor and fruit that will echo the menu's sweet-sour contrasts: a rich Chardonnay from Australia or America or a dry Gewürztraminer. The red wine should be full-bodied, but not heady: a fresh Pinot Noir or a Cabernet blend. With dessert, offer chilled plum brandy.

Wildflowers and vine trimmings are casually arranged in a large vase or pitcher to form the centerpiece. Left, a watering can becomes an impromptu vase for seasonal blossoms for a side table. Clusters of grapes are an edible embellishment.

PREPARATION LIST

• Several months ahead, prepare the chutney (commercial chutney may be substituted).

• Up to 1 week ahead, make the cherry tomato sauce for the eggplant.

• The day before, wrap and oil the cheese.

• The night before, marinate the lamb.

• The morning of the lunch, bake the focaccia; make the lentil salad and the plum tart.

• One hour before, let the lamb come to room temperature before grilling.

EACH RECIPE YIELDS 6 SERVINGS

Bottles of a favorite vintage, adorned with flowers and homemade name tags, make ideal gifts for guests.

GRILLED PEPPERED FIGS WITH GRILLED GOAT CHEESE IN GRAPE LEAVES

SERVES 6

The sweetest figs of all are often the cracked, homely looking ones. When figs are not in season, substitute peaches or good, juicy pears.

six 1-inch-thick (2.5-cm) slices mild fresh goat cheese
6 bottled grape leaves, rinsed of brine and stemmed
6 large ripe figs
6 thin slices prosciutto
olive oil for brushing
freshly ground pepper to taste
6 lime wedges

Wrap each slice of goat cheese in a grape leaf, folding in the ends and sides so it resembles a neat packet. If made ahead, cover and refrigerate overnight.
❧ Prepare a fire in a grill. Position the oiled rack 4–6 inches (10–15 cm) above the fire. Or, preheat a broiler (griller).
❧ Cut each fig in half lengthwise. Cut the prosciutto slices in half lengthwise. Wrap each fig half with a piece of prosciutto and thread 2 halves on each of 6 skewers. Brush the wrapped figs and cheese lightly with olive oil and sprinkle with pepper.
❧ Cook the figs and cheese on the grill over medium-hot coals or broil until figs are heated through (about 3 minutes) and the cheese is soft and warm (about 4 minutes), turning once. Divide the figs and cheese among 6 small plates and garnish each with a lime wedge.

WALNUT FOCACCIA

MAKES ONE 11- BY 18-INCH
(28- BY 46-CM) FOCACCIA

Add grapes to this hearty bread if you are not serving the figs in the same menu. Toasted walnut oil is richer in flavor than pale, untoasted varieties.

FOR THE DOUGH:
2 teaspoons active dry yeast
1¼ cups (10 fl oz/300 ml) warm (110°F/43°C) water
2 tablespoons sugar
3¾ cups (19 oz/595 g) unbleached all-purpose (plain) flour
3 tablespoons toasted walnut oil
1 teaspoon salt

FOR THE TOPPING:
toasted walnut oil
1 cup (4 oz/125 g) chopped toasted walnuts (see glossary)
2 tablespoons minced fresh rosemary
2 cups (10 oz/315 g) halved and seeded red grapes, optional
1–2 tablespoons sugar, optional

PHOTOGRAPH BY PETER JOHNSON

Newly harvested grapes, cut from the vines with a traditional knife, wait in a wooden lug to go to the winepress.

To make the dough, dissolve the yeast in ½ cup (8 fl oz/250 ml) of the warm water in the bowl of an electric mixer. Add the sugar and ½ cup (2½ oz/75 g) of the flour and mix to combine. Cover and let sit for about 30 minutes. Add the remaining flour, the remaining water, the walnut oil and the salt and mix well. Beat on low speed with the dough hook attached until the dough leaves the bowl cleanly, about 10 minutes. Or, mix the dough in a food processor until well combined. Then turn out onto a lightly floured board and knead until the dough is smooth and elastic, about 10 minutes, adding more flour if necessary to prevent sticking. Transfer the dough to an oiled bowl, cover with a kitchen towel and let rise in a warm place until doubled, about 1 hour.
❧ Preheat an oven to 475°F (240°C). Punch down the dough and turn it out on a lightly floured board. Form into an 11- by 18-inch (28- by 46-cm) rectangle and place in a sided baking pan of the same dimensions. Cover the dough loosely and allow it to rest until doubled, about 15–30 minutes.
❧ To make the topping, brush the dough lightly with walnut oil, then dimple the top with your fingers. Sprinkle with the walnuts and rosemary. (If using grapes, push them into the dough and sprinkle the focaccia with the sugar, then add the walnuts and rosemary.) Bake on the lower rack of the oven until golden brown on top, about 12–15 minutes.

Grilled Peppered Figs with Grilled Goat Cheese in Grape Leaves; Walnut Focaccia

BUTTERFLIED LEG OF LAMB IN MIDDLE EASTERN YOGURT MARINADE

SERVES 6

A butterflied leg of lamb has thick and thin portions, yielding both rare and medium meat. The very simple marinade produces spectacular results.

1 large leg of lamb, about 6 lb (3 kg), boned, butterflied and trimmed of fat and silverskin
1 large onion, chopped
2–3 cloves garlic, minced
½ teaspoon ground cinnamon
½ teaspoon ground cardamom
¼ teaspoon saffron threads, crushed
1 teaspoon ground ginger or 1 table-spoon grated fresh ginger
1 tablespoon ground coriander
½ teaspoon freshly ground pepper
2 cups (1 lb/500 g) plain lowfat or nonfat yogurt
3 tablespoons fresh lemon juice
½ cup (¾ oz/20 g) chopped fresh mint
oil for brushing
salt and freshly ground pepper to taste

*P*lace the butterflied lamb leg in a glass or plastic container large enough to hold it in one layer. Set aside.
&❧ Place the onion and garlic in a food processor or blender and pulse until coarsely chopped. Add the cinnamon, cardamom, saffron, ginger, coriander, pepper, yogurt, lemon juice and mint and purée. Pour over the lamb, cover and marinate overnight in the refrigerator, turning occasionally.

Butterflied Leg of Lamb in Middle Eastern Yogurt Marinade; Spiced Apricot Chutney; Grilled Eggplant with Sweet Cherry Tomato Sauce

PHOTOGRAPH BY PETER JOHNSON

~ Prepare a fire in a grill. Position the oiled rack 4–6 inches (10–15 cm) above the fire. Or, preheat a broiler (griller).

~ Remove the lamb from the marinade. Brush with oil and sprinkle with salt and pepper. Grill over medium-hot coals or broil for 8–10 minutes on each side for rare, or 12 minutes for medium rare. The thicker section may take a few minutes longer. Slice across the grain to serve.

SPICED APRICOT CHUTNEY

MAKES ABOUT 6 CUPS (48 OZ/1.5 KG)

Sweet-tart apricots have an affinity for lamb. Make the chutney when the fruit is in season and let it sit in a cool, dark place for 2–3 weeks to mellow the flavors before using. Or, substitute commercial chutney.

6 cups (1½ lb/750 g) pitted and
   quartered fresh apricots
2 cups (1 lb/500 g) sugar
½ tablespoon salt
1 onion, chopped
one 4- by 1½-inch (10- by 4-cm)
   piece fresh ginger, peeled and sliced
3 cloves garlic
1 teaspoon ground cinnamon
½ teaspoon ground cloves
½ teaspoon cayenne pepper or 3–4
   jalapeño (hot green) chili peppers,
   minced
1½ cups (12 fl oz/375 ml)
   cider vinegar

*P*lace the apricots in a large, heavy enameled or stainless-steel pot. Cover with the sugar and salt and let stand for at least 1 hour or up to 8 hours.

~ In a food processor or blender, pulse or blend the onion, ginger, garlic, cinnamon, cloves and cayenne or

chilies until chopped. Add half of the vinegar and purée. Pour this mixture over the apricots and stir in the remaining vinegar. Bring to a boil, then reduce heat and simmer, uncovered and stirring often, until the mixture is thick and a teaspoonful sets up on a chilled plate, about 1 hour. Pour into 3 hot sterilized 2-cup (16–fl oz/500-ml) canning jars, leaving about ½ inch (12 mm) of head space, then seal the jars. Process in a hot-water bath for 10 minutes (see Canning, page 186) or store in the refrigerator for up to 3 months.

GRILLED EGGPLANT WITH SWEET CHERRY TOMATO SAUCE

SERVES 6

The sauce, more like a conserve, is also excellent on cream cheese, goat cheese or grilled chicken.

FOR THE CHERRY TOMATO SAUCE:
2 cups (12 oz/375 g) stemmed
   cherry tomatoes
½ cup (3½ oz/105 g) light brown
   sugar, packed
grated zest of 1 lemon
¼ cup (2 fl oz/60 ml) fresh
   lemon juice
1 tablespoon grated fresh ginger
3 tablespoons water
½ teaspoon ground cinnamon
½ teaspoon ground cumin
pinch of cayenne pepper
salt and freshly ground pepper to taste

FOR THE GRILLED EGGPLANT:
1 clove garlic, crushed
¼ cup (2 fl oz/60 ml) olive oil,
   slightly warmed
2 firm globe eggplants (aubergines),
   about ½–¾ lb (250–375 g) each, or
   6 slender (Asian) eggplants (aubergines)
salt and freshly ground pepper to taste

*T*o make the sauce, combine the tomatoes, brown sugar, lemon zest, lemon juice, ginger, water, cinnamon, cumin and cayenne in a saucepan. Cook, uncovered, over moderate heat, stirring occasionally, until the tomatoes break down and the mixture becomes thick and syrupy, about 30 minutes. Season with salt and pepper and transfer to a bowl or jar. If desired, cover and refrigerate up to 1 week. Makes about 1 cup (8 fl oz/250 ml).

~ To make the grilled eggplant, steep the garlic in the warm olive oil for about 1 hour. Prepare a fire in a grill. Position the oiled rack 4–6 inches (10–15 cm) above the fire. Or, preheat a broiler (griller). Peel the globe eggplants and slice them 1 inch thick (2.5 cm) crosswise. If using slender eggplants, do not peel; cut each in half lengthwise and score the top with the point of a knife. Brush the eggplants with the garlic oil and sprinkle with salt and pepper. Grill or broil the eggplant, turning once, until soft but not too browned, about 3 minutes on each side.

~ Meanwhile, rewarm the tomato sauce over low heat. When the eggplants are done, divide the slices among 6 plates (or place 2 halves of slender eggplant on each), top with the tomato sauce and serve.

PHOTOGRAPH BY PETER JOHNSON

Lentil Salad

LENTIL SALAD

SERVES 6

For the best texture, make the salad no more than several hours in advance. If you make it ahead, fold in half the mint, adding the rest before serving.

2 cups (14 oz/440 g) green or
   brown lentils
1 bay leaf
1 teaspoon salt
½ cup (4 fl oz/125 ml) plus 3 tablespoons olive oil
¼ cup (2 fl oz/60 ml) fresh
   lemon juice
2 cups (8 oz/250 g) diced onions
1 teaspoon minced garlic
2 tablespoons ground cumin
1 teaspoon ground coriander
grated zest of 1 lemon
½ cup (¾ oz/20 g) chopped
   fresh mint
salt and freshly ground pepper to taste

Place the lentils and bay leaf in a deep saucepan and cover with cold water to a depth of 3 inches (7.5 cm) above the lentils. Bring to a boil over high heat, add the salt, reduce heat and simmer, covered, until the lentils are tender but still firm. Green lentils can take as long as 45 minutes, brown as few as 15, so keep testing. When the lentils are done, drain off any excess water, toss the lentils in the ½ cup (4 fl oz/125 ml) olive oil and the lemon juice and set aside.

❧ Heat the remaining 3 tablespoons oil in a large sauté pan, add the onions and cook until tender and translucent, about 10 minutes. Add the garlic, cumin, coriander and lemon zest and cook 2–3 minutes longer. Add the cooked onion mixture to the lentils. Fold in the mint and season with salt and pepper. Serve at room temperature.

PHOTOGRAPH BY PETER JOHNSON

Blue Plum Tart

BLUE PLUM TART

*Plum and citrus flavors predominate in
this nutty tart. Substitute other varieties
of plums for the prune plums if necessary.*

basic pie pastry for a single-crust pie
shell (recipe on page 177)
½ cup (2 oz/60 g) plus 2 tablespoons
hazelnuts, toasted and skinned
(see glossary)
½ cup (4 oz/125 g) plus 2
tablespoons sugar
½ teaspoon ground cinnamon
½ teaspoon ground ginger
3 tablespoons unsalted butter at
room temperature

16–20 Italian prune plums, halved
and pitted
¾ cup (6 fl oz/180 ml) orange
marmalade
whipped cream flavored with about 1
teaspoon grated orange zest, optional

Preheat an oven to 400°F (200°C).
Roll out the pastry into a large rectangle
on a lightly floured surface. Use to
line an 8- by 11-inch (20- by 28-cm)
rectangular tart pan or a 10-inch
(25-cm) round tart pan. Set aside in the
freezer while you make the filling.
ఈ Finely chop the ½ cup (2 oz/60 g)
hazelnuts and coarsely chop the remaining 2 tablespoons hazelnuts. Combine
the finely chopped hazelnuts, the ½ cup
(4 oz/125 g) sugar, cinnamon, ginger
and butter in a food processor or a

medium bowl; pulse or cut in the butter
with a pastry cutter or 2 knives until
blended into a paste. Press onto the
bottom of the pastry-lined tart pan. Top
with the plums, arranged in overlapping
rows. Sprinkle with the remaining 2
tablespoons sugar and bake on the middle
rack of the oven for 10 minutes. Reduce
the heat to 350°F (180°C) and bake
until the plums are bubbly and the crust
is golden, about 20–30 minutes more.
ఈ Meanwhile, melt the orange marmalade in a small saucepan; strain and keep
warm. When the tart is done, brush the
marmalade over the plums and sprinkle
with the 2 tablespoons coarsely chopped
hazelnuts. If desired, serve each piece
with a dollop of orange-flavored
whipped cream.

Pre-Theater Cocktails

When groups of friends gather together to attend an evening event such as a play, opera or dance performance, dinner can pose a challenge. With curtain-up usually between 7 and 8 p.m., there is often too little time for a sit-down meal. That is when a cocktail party makes such perfect sense, not just before a show but for any occasion when you want to entertain guests without extending the party into a full night's event.

We set our cocktail party in a living room with a lovely city view, but a den or library anywhere is also appropriate. Because of the relaxed style of this gathering, we decorated the room simply by placing seasonal foliage and fruit in various spots. The owner's collection of memorabilia served as the ideal backdrop.

Menu

Greek Chicken Strudel

*Roasted Peppers
with Herbed Goat Cheese*

Tomato Tart

Roasted Eggplant Salad

Crab Salad in Endive Leaves

Baked Clams Oreganati

*Mushrooms Stuffed
with Sweet Sausage*

The array of finger foods and small dishes selected for this cock-tail party for twelve offers something to please everyone. The portions are generous enough to keep appetites at bay all evening. Autumn flavors predominate, since fall is when many arts seasons begin, but you can make these recipes any time of year. Most dishes can be prepared at least partly in advance, with minimal cleanup.

Try placing platters of food with plenty of small plates, cutlery and cocktail napkins at various convenient spots around the room where guests can serve themselves. Likewise, you might want to arrange separate stations for a self-service wine bar and a full liquor bar with ready-to-mix cocktails and mineral water. In so doing, you'll establish different conversation areas and encourage guests to mingle.

WINE RECOMMENDATIONS

Offer a choice of white and red wines. For the white, select one with a pronounced flavor to accent the sharper tastes of the food: a classic Sauvignon Blanc or a Pinot Gris from Oregon or Alsace. Choose a well-concentrated red with earthy overtones: a Cabernet Sauvignon or a high-quality Beaujolais, such as a Moulin à Vent or a Morgon.

An elegant silver tray with premium liquors, ice bucket, cocktail shaker and assorted glasses transforms a sideboard into a self-service bar. Left, seasonal foliage and fruits, such as colorful autumn leaves and persimmons, add a simple, classic decorative flourish.

PREPARATION LIST

• The morning of the party, make the eggplant salad; stuff and refrigerate the mushrooms.

• Three to 4 hours ahead, assemble and slice the peppers with goat cheese and cover with plastic wrap; steam and open clams, top with bread crumbs, cover and refrigerate.

• One to 2 hours ahead, bake the tart, to be gently rewarmed at serving time or served at room temperature; prepare the crab in endive.

THIS MENU SERVES 12 GENEROUSLY FOR COCKTAILS. FOR A SMALLER GROUP, SERVE FEWER DISHES.

On a side table, an arrangement of wine bottles, glasses and cocktail napkins allows guests to serve themselves.

GREEK CHICKEN STRUDEL

MAKES 3 STRUDELS

This recipe is also excellent as a light main course for supper. If you prefer, you could layer the filo and filling in lasagna pans, then slice into wedges to serve.

FOR THE FILLING:

about 3 cups (24 fl oz/750 ml)
   chicken stock
6 boneless, skinless chicken breast halves
6 cups (12 oz/375 g) loosely packed
   chopped spinach leaves, well washed
3 tablespoons olive oil
1½ cups (5 oz/155 g) minced green
   (spring) onions
⅓ cup (½ oz/15 g) chopped fresh dill
⅓ cup (½ oz/15 g) chopped fresh parsley
¾ lb (375 g) feta cheese, crumbled,
   about 2½ cups
5 oz (155 g) Monterey jack cheese,
   grated, about 1¼ cups
3 eggs
½ teaspoon freshly grated nutmeg
1 teaspoon ground coriander
¼ teaspoon cayenne pepper
¾ cup (3 oz/90 g) chopped toasted
   walnuts (see glossary)
salt and freshly ground pepper to taste

FOR ASSEMBLY:

12 sheets filo pastry
⅓–½ cup (3–4 oz/90–125 g)
   unsalted butter, melted, for brushing

To make the filling, bring enough stock to cover the chicken breasts to a boil in a wide sauté pan. Add the breasts, reduce the heat and poach, uncovered, until the chicken is cooked through, about 8–10 minutes. Lift out and let cool, then shred or chop the meat. Save the stock for another recipe.
❧ Place the spinach with the water clinging to it in a large frying pan and stir over medium heat until wilted, about 3 minutes. Drain well and squeeze dry.
❧ Heat the oil in a sauté pan, add the green onions and cook until soft, about 5 minutes. Place in a bowl with the chicken, spinach, dill, parsley, feta cheese, jack cheese, eggs, nutmeg, coriander, cayenne and walnuts; stir until well combined. Season liberally with salt and pepper.
❧ Preheat an oven to 325°F (170°C). To assemble the strudels, brush a sheet of filo with the melted butter. Place another sheet on top, brush again, repeat for 2 more layers, then place a thin row of chicken mixture along the long side. Tuck in the ends and roll up. Repeat until all the filling and filo is used up; you will have 3 strudels. Transfer to baking sheets and bake on the middle rack of the oven until golden brown, about 25–30 minutes. Allow to rest for 10 minutes, then cut into 1-inch (2.5-cm) slices crosswise with a serrated knife.

A quiet corner provides comfortable seating.

ROASTED PEPPERS WITH HERBED GOAT CHEESE

MAKES ABOUT 72 APPETIZERS

Resembling colorful pinwheels, this simple hors d'oeuvre combines the rich, creamy tang of goat cheese with the sweetness of bell peppers.

6 large red bell peppers (capsicums) or
   pimiento peppers (capsicums)
1¼ lb (625 g) fresh mild goat cheese,
   crumbled, about 4 cups
¼ cup (⅜ oz/10 g) chopped
   fresh chives
¼ cup (⅜ oz/10 g) chopped
   fresh parsley
2 cloves garlic, minced
2 teaspoons chopped fresh thyme
3 tablespoons chopped fresh basil
grated zest of 1 lemon
½ teaspoon freshly ground pepper
pinch of cayenne pepper
heavy (double) cream, optional
fresh thyme sprigs, optional

Roast, peel and derib the peppers as directed on page 189. Try to keep the peppers in unbroken halves.
❧ In a bowl, mix well the cheese, chives, parsley, garlic, thyme, basil, lemon zest and ground pepper; season to taste with cayenne. Add a bit of cream if the cheese mixture is very stiff and difficult to mix. Spread the cheese mixture onto the pepper halves and roll them into cylinders lengthwise. Refrigerate for a few hours to firm the filling.
❧ At serving time, cut each pepper roll crosswise into about 6 rounds. Arrange on a platter and garnish with the thyme sprigs, if using.

*Greek Chicken Strudel;
Roasted Peppers with Herbed Goat Cheese*

TOMATO TART

MAKES 12 SERVINGS

Similar to a quiche, this French-style tart could be given an Italian flair by substituting basil for the mint and mozzarella for the Gruyère.

basic pie pastry for a single-crust pie
   shell (recipe on page 177)
3 large tomatoes, cut into ½-inch-
   thick (12-mm) slices
salt to taste
2 tablespoons Dijon mustard
3 tablespoons chopped fresh mint
4 oz (125 g) Gruyère or Emmenthaler
   cheese, cut into 8 thin slices
2 eggs
1 cup (8 fl oz/250 ml) heavy
   (double) cream
freshly ground pepper to taste

*R*oll out the pastry and use it to line a 10-inch (25-cm) pie or tart pan. Set it aside in the freezer for 30 minutes.

With your fingers, carefully push out the seeds and watery juices from the tomato slices. Sprinkle the sliced tomatoes with salt and place in a large colander to drain. After 30 minutes, remove the tomatoes from the colander and pat them dry.

Preheat an oven to 350°F (180°C). With a rubber spatula, spread the mustard over the bottom of the tart shell and sprinkle the chopped mint over the mustard. Top with the cheese, then place the tomato slices over the cheese. In a small bowl, beat together the eggs and cream, season with salt and pepper and pour over the tomatoes. Bake until pale gold and the custard is set, about 30 minutes. Let rest for 10 minutes, then slice and serve.

ROASTED EGGPLANT SALAD

MAKES 12 SERVINGS

If you make this low-fat salad ahead of time, wait until just before serving to fold in the mint and almonds.

3 large globe eggplants (aubergines)
1 cup (8 oz/250 g) plain nonfat yogurt
2 tablespoons fresh lemon juice or
   to taste
1 tablespoon minced garlic
1 teaspoon minced jalapeño (hot green)
   chili pepper or more to taste
2 teaspoons ground cumin
salt and freshly ground pepper to taste
⅔ cup (3 oz/90 g) toasted almonds
   (see glossary), chopped
¼ cup (⅜ oz/10 g) chopped fresh mint
4 pita bread rounds, cut into 6
   wedges each

*P*reheat an oven to 400°F (200°C). Place the eggplants on a baking sheet and prick all over with a fork. Roast, turning occasionally for even cooking, until the eggplants are soft and tender, about 1 hour. Remove from the oven and let sit until cool enough to handle. Peel the eggplant and place the pulp in a colander to drain for about 30 minutes.

Place the eggplant pulp in a food processor or blender and pulse to purée. Add the yogurt, lemon juice, garlic, jalapeño and cumin. Pulse quickly to mix. Add salt and pepper. Transfer the purée to a serving bowl. If desired, cover and refrigerate for up to 6 hours. Stir in the chopped toasted almonds and mint and serve with the pita wedges.

Tomato Tart; Roasted Eggplant Salad

CRAB SALAD IN ENDIVE LEAVES

MAKES 24 APPETIZERS

The crisp, slightly bitter endive contrasts nicely with the mild sweetness of the crab. Substitute small romaine leaves if you like.

grated zest of 1 lemon
2 tablespoons lemon juice
1 teaspoon chopped fresh tarragon
2 tablespoons chopped fresh chives
2 tablespoons chopped fresh parsley
1 tablespoon Dijon mustard
½ cup (4 fl oz/125 ml) mayonnaise or
    as needed to bind
1 lb (500 g) fresh crab meat, picked
    over and any cartilage removed
¾ cup (4 oz/125 g) diced celery
salt, freshly ground pepper and cayenne
    pepper to taste
24 Belgian endive (chicory/witloof) leaves

*I*n a bowl, combine the lemon zest, lemon juice, tarragon, chives, parsley, mustard and mayonnaise; mix well. Stir in the crab and celery and season with salt, ground pepper and cayenne. Cover and refrigerate up to 6 hours. To serve, spoon the crab mixture into the endive leaves and chill for at least 30 minutes or up to 2 hours to firm the filling.

A slice of tomato tart, a glass of wine and an inviting chair await a guest.

BAKED CLAMS OREGANATI

MAKES 36 APPETIZERS

When preparing live clams, tap each one to be sure the shells close tightly.

36 Manila or littleneck clams, scrubbed
dry white wine
3 tablespoons olive oil
2 cloves garlic, minced
1 tablespoon dried oregano
½ cup (2 oz/60 g) dried bread crumbs
1 tablespoon chopped fresh parsley
3 tablespoons freshly grated Parmesan
    cheese, optional
salt and freshly ground pepper to taste
rock salt
lemon wedges

*P*lace the clams in a large sauté pan with about 1 inch (2.5 cm) of white wine. Cover the pan and steam over high heat just until the clams open, 2–8 minutes. Remove from the heat immediately and, using a slotted spoon, transfer the clams to a platter; discard any unopened clams. Remove the top shells and discard. Loosen each clam from its bottom shell with a knife so that it can be picked up easily. Strain the juices in the pan and reserve.
❧ Warm the olive oil in a small sauté pan, add the garlic and oregano and cook over low heat for 2 minutes. Remove from the heat and stir in the bread crumbs, parsley and Parmesan, if desired. Let cool. Sprinkle the bread crumbs over the clams and drizzle with a few drops of the reserved pan juices. Season with salt and pepper. Cover and refrigerate until serving time.
❧ To serve, preheat a broiler (griller). Arrange the clams on a rock salt–lined baking pan that can fit under the broiler. Broil the clams until browned on top, about 5 minutes. Serve with lemons.

MUSHROOMS STUFFED WITH SWEET SAUSAGE

MAKES 24 APPETIZERS

You can stuff and refrigerate the mushroom caps the morning of the party.

24 large fresh mushrooms
4 tablespoons (2 fl oz/60 ml) oil
½ cup (2 oz/60 g) chopped onion
1 tablespoon minced garlic
½ lb (250 g) ground pork
½ teaspoon ground cinnamon
¼ teaspoon ground nutmeg
1 teaspoon toasted fennel seed, ground
    (see glossary)
1 tablespoon grated orange zest
¼ cup (1 oz/30 g) dried bread crumbs
salt and freshly ground pepper to taste
1 cup (8 fl oz/250 ml) chicken stock

*R*emove the stems from the mushrooms and chop them; reserve the caps. Heat 2 tablespoons of the oil in a large sauté pan. Add the chopped onion and cook until soft, about 5 minutes. Add the chopped stems and cook over high heat until they start to become dry, about 5 minutes. Stir in the garlic and cook for 1 minute. Transfer to a bowl and set the mixture aside.
❧ Heat the remaining 2 tablespoons of oil in the same pan. Cook the pork, breaking it up with a fork, until it is no longer pink, about 5 minutes. Stir in the cinnamon, nutmeg, fennel seed and orange zest. Add the cooked mushroom and onion mixture and the bread crumbs; mix well. Season with salt and pepper and adjust the rest of the spices.
❧ Preheat the oven to 350°F (180°C). Stuff the pork mixture into the mushroom caps. Place the mushrooms in a baking pan and drizzle the stock around them. Bake until cooked through, about 20–25 minutes. Serve warm.

Baked Clams Oreganati; Mushrooms Stuffed with Sweet Sausage; Crab Salad in Endive Leaves

MEDITERRANEAN EASTER

Easter is a joyous holiday in the Mediterranean, where it is usually celebrated with a midday or evening feast laden with symbols of the birth of a new season. Crisp greens, fresh seafood, tender spring lamb, fragrant herbs, plump eggplants and artichokes, sweet honey and rich nuts and cheese—each is a gift from the reawakening earth and each finds its way onto the Mediterranean Easter table.

For our holiday meal, we chose the dining room of a charming home with views of the surrounding hillsides. We set the table with handmade glazed pottery to complement the earthy food. To bring springtime sights and scents indoors, we decorated the room with bundles and bouquets of herbs and terra-cotta pots of fresh oregano, thyme and rosemary. Look for these in vegetable shops, farmer's markets and garden nurseries.

Menu

Gypsy Spinach Pie

———

Salmon Dolmas with Avgolemono

———

*Rack of Spring Lamb Marinated in
Garlic, Allspice, Cumin & Thyme*

Artichoke Hearts with Tomatoes & Currants

Stuffed Eggplant

Asparagus & Potatoes with Almonds & Mint

———

Citrus & Honey Cheesecake with Nut Crust

You don't have to observe the holiday to enjoy this Easter repast; it requires only a desire to celebrate the season. The food for this meal is perfect for family-style serving, with everything passed informally on platters at the table. Place wines on a nearby sideboard, ready to open and share as the meal progresses.

For a traditional Easter symbol, try dyeing eggs using a natural, old-fashioned method. First, bring yellow onion skins to a boil in a saucepan of water to make a russet-colored dye; let the liquid cool. Then, form a pattern on the eggshells with thin strips of masking tape. Dip the eggs into the dye and let them dry on a rack before peeling off the tape to reveal the pattern. Or display small, mottled quail eggs, found in specialty food shops.

WINE RECOMMENDATIONS

With the spinach pie, serve a Sauvignon Blanc from Chile, France or California, or a moderately rich Italian Soave. With the salmon, pour a dry Chenin Blanc or a Washington State Riesling. For the lamb, offer a hearty, rich Italian red such as Barolo, or an American Merlot. With dessert, serve a cream or brown sherry.

Small pots of Mediterranean herbs surround a place setting with fragrances of the new season. Left, on a side patio, two rustic chairs could provide a couple of guests with a quiet spot for conversation.

PREPARATION LIST

• Up to 2 days ahead, start marinating the lamb.

• The day before, make the artichokes and the eggplant; re-warm the artichokes on the stovetop and the eggplant in the oven just before serving.

• The morning of the party, bake the cheesecake.

• Up to 4 hours ahead, make the spinach pie; roast the potatoes and blanch the asparagus.

• Two to 3 hours in advance, assemble the dolmas; bake them and prepare the sauce just before serving.

EACH RECIPE YIELDS 6 SERVINGS AND CAN EASILY BE DOUBLED TO SERVE 12 AS SHOWN.

Crackled glasses filled with Spanish Sherry are offered with dessert.

GYPSY SPINACH PIE

MAKES ONE 9-INCH (23-CM) PIE (6 SERVINGS)

This robust two-crust pie also makes a nice lunch on its own. To serve twelve, make two pies as shown.

basic pie pastry for a double-crust pie
   shell (recipe on page 177)
2 lb (1 kg) spinach (about 4 bunches),
   washed well and stemmed; or a
   mixture of spinach, beet (beetroot)
   greens, sorrel and Swiss chard
   (silverbeet), about 8–9 cups; or two
   10-oz (315 g) packages frozen
   chopped spinach, thawed
¼ cup (2 oz/60 g) unsalted butter or
   olive oil (2 fl oz/60 ml)
2 bunches green (spring) onions, chopped
2 tablespoons all-purpose (plain) flour
salt and pepper to taste
¼ teaspoon ground nutmeg, or
   to taste
⅛ teaspoon cayenne pepper
¼ cup (1 oz/30 g) toasted pine nuts
   (see glossary)
½ cup (3 oz/90 g) dried currants,
   soaked in warm water for 10 minutes
½ cup (¾ oz/20 g) chopped
   fresh parsley
½ cup (¾ oz/20 g) chopped
   fresh dill
4 hard-cooked eggs
¼ cup (1 oz/30 g) toasted bread crumbs
olive oil for brushing

Preheat an oven to 375°F (190°C).
Roll out the pastry for the bottom crust
and use it to line a 9-inch (23-cm) pie
pan. Roll out the pastry for the top
crust and set it aside.
❧ Place the spinach or greens with the
water clinging to the leaves in a large
frying pan and stir over medium heat

Gypsy Spinach Pie

until wilted, about 3 minutes. Drain well, chop coarsely and squeeze as dry as possible.

ᦉ Heat the butter or oil in a small sauté pan. Add the green onions and cook until soft, about 3 minutes. Stir in the flour and cook 2–3 minutes longer. Add this mixture to the chopped greens and season well with salt, pepper, nutmeg and cayenne. Fold in the pine nuts, drained currants, parsley and dill. Slice the hard-cooked eggs.

ᦉ Sprinkle the bread crumbs in a layer in the bottom of the pastry-lined pie pan, then add the greens mixture. Top with the sliced eggs. Brush the edge of the bottom crust with water, place the top crust on the pie and trim the excess dough, then crimp the edges together. Cut a steam hole in the center of the top crust and decorate the top with the pastry trimmings. Brush the crust top with olive oil and bake on the middle rack of the oven until golden, about 40 minutes. Remove from the oven and let rest for 10 minutes before slicing.

SALMON DOLMAS WITH AVGOLEMONO

SERVES 6

In traditional dolmas, a rice filling is wrapped in the grape leaves and fresh lemon juice is squeezed over the top.

1⅛ lb (560 g) salmon fillet, skinned
12 bottled grape leaves, rinsed of brine and stemmed
1 cup (8 fl oz/250 ml) fish stock or chicken stock
2 eggs, separated
2 tablespoons fresh lemon juice
freshly ground pepper to taste
chopped fresh dill
lemon wedges

Preheat an oven to 450°F (230°C). Cut the salmon into twelve 1½-oz (45-g) strips, each about 2½ inches (6 cm) long and 1½ inches (4 cm) wide. Wrap each piece in a grape leaf. Place the dolmas seam-side down in a shallow baking pan. Drizzle the fish stock or chicken stock over the dolmas and bake until the fish is firm but not mushy, about 4–5 minutes.

ᦉ Meanwhile, in a bowl, beat the egg yolks and lemon juice together until frothy. In a separate bowl, beat the egg whites until soft peaks form and fold them into the yolks.

ᦉ Remove the dolmas to warm individual plates. Pour the stock into a small sauté pan. Add the egg mixture to the warm stock, whisking constantly until thickened, 1–2 minutes. Pour the sauce over the dolmas, sprinkle with pepper and the chopped dill and serve at once, garnished with lemon wedges.

Salmon Dolmas with Avgolemono

Rack of Spring Lamb Marinated in Garlic, Allspice, Cumin & Thyme; Stuffed Eggplant; Artichoke Hearts with Tomatoes & Currants; Asparagus & Potatoes with Almonds & Mint (page 108)

RACK OF SPRING LAMB MARINATED IN GARLIC, ALLSPICE, CUMIN & THYME

SERVES 6

The marinade combines Greek, Turkish and North African flavors. For twelve guests, double the recipe as shown.

FOR THE MARINADE:

1 onion, grated
2 tablespoons minced garlic
3 tablespoons fresh lemon juice
grated zest of 1 lemon and 1 orange
1 tablespoon Dijon mustard
1 teaspoon ground allspice
2 teaspoons ground cumin
½ teaspoon cayenne pepper
2 tablespoons chopped fresh thyme
  leaves, or 2 teaspoons dried thyme
1 teaspoon freshly ground pepper
½ cup (4 fl oz/125 ml) olive oil

FOR THE LAMB:

2 racks of lamb, trimmed, or 12
  lamb chops
oil for brushing chops
salt to taste for chops

To make the marinade, combine the onion, garlic, lemon juice, lemon zest, orange zest, mustard, allspice, cumin, cayenne, thyme and ground pepper in a food processor or blender. Pulse or blend to purée. Gradually add the olive oil until the mixture is blended.

❧ Place the lamb in a glass or plastic container and coat the meat with the marinade. Cover and refrigerate for at least 6 hours or up to 2 days.

❧ To cook the racks, preheat an oven to 350°F (180°C). Sear the racks in a cast-iron frying pan over high heat or on a hot griddle until browned on all sides, then transfer to a roasting pan and roast in the oven until a meat thermometer inserted in the center of a rack reads 125°F (52°C), about 10–12 minutes. Let the lamb rest for 10 minutes on a carving board, covered with aluminum foil, before slicing; meat will be medium rare.

❧ To cook the chops instead, preheat a broiler (griller). Or, prepare a fire in a grill and position the oiled grill rack 4–6 inches (10–15 cm) above the fire. Brush the chops with oil, sprinkle with salt and broil or grill them for 3 minutes on each side for rare, or 4 minutes on each side for medium rare.

ARTICHOKE HEARTS WITH TOMATOES & CURRANTS

SERVES 6

Sweet-sour artichoke preparations such as this one are common in the Mediterranean.

6 large (about 4-inch/10-cm diameter) artichokes
1 lemon half
2 tablespoons fresh lemon juice
¼ cup (2 fl oz/60 ml) olive oil
1 cup (8 fl oz/250 ml) water, stock or dry white wine
2 cups (12 oz/375 g) peeled, diced tomatoes or drained and chopped canned plum tomatoes
½ cup (3 oz/90 g) dried currants, soaked in warm water to cover for 10 minutes
2 tablespoons honey
salt and freshly ground pepper to taste

*C*ut the stems and tops off of the artichokes, break off and discard most of the outer leaves and remove all the rest with a sharp knife. Scoop out the fuzzy chokes with a small sharp spoon. Rub the cut surfaces with the lemon half and float the artichoke hearts in a bowl of cold water mixed with the lemon juice until all the artichokes

are prepared. Drain and pat dry just before cooking.

❧ Pour the olive oil into a large sauté pan and place over medium-high heat. Add the artichoke hearts and toss them to coat with the oil and add the water, stock or wine. Cover the pan and steam until the artichoke hearts are tender-crisp, about 12–15 minutes (most of the liquid will have been absorbed). Add the tomatoes, drained currants and honey; stir well and simmer, uncovered, until the artichokes are tender when pierced with a knife and the pan juices have reduced, about 10 minutes longer. Season with salt and pepper and add more honey or lemon juice if desired. Transfer the artichoke hearts to a platter and spoon the sauce on top.

STUFFED EGGPLANT

SERVES 6

Be sure to precook the eggplant shells to make them tender and completely edible.

3 baby globe eggplants (aubergines) or 6 slender (Asian) eggplants (aubergines)
salt
½ cup (4 fl oz/125 ml) plus 2 tablespoons olive oil
1 large onion, chopped
4 large cloves garlic, minced
1 tablespoon dried oregano
1½ cups (9 oz/280 g) peeled, diced tomatoes
¼ cup (⅜ oz/10 g) chopped fresh parsley
freshly ground pepper to taste
½ cup (4 fl oz/125 ml) water

*C*ut the eggplants in half lengthwise. With a sharp knife, carefully score the flesh and remove most of the eggplant pulp, leaving a shell that is ¼ inch (6 mm) thick. Dice the pulp and set aside. Salt the eggplant shells and let sit,

flesh sides down, in a colander for 1 hour, then rinse and pat dry.

❧ Preheat an oven to 350°F (180°C). Warm 2 tablespoons of the olive oil in a large sauté pan. Add the onion and cook until tender and translucent, about 10 minutes. Set aside in a bowl. In the same pan, heat 6 tablespoons (3 fl oz/90 ml) of the olive oil, add the diced eggplant and cook until softened, about 5 minutes. Stir in the garlic, oregano and tomatoes and simmer for about 3 minutes. Add the onion and parsley to this mixture. Season to taste with salt and pepper and set aside.

❧ Heat the remaining 2 tablespoons of the oil in a large sauté pan and cook the eggplant shells, turning once or twice, for a few minutes to soften them. Then place them side by side in an oiled baking dish and stuff with the reserved filling. Add the water to the pan, cover and bake until very tender, about 45 minutes.

*P*lant a selection of Mediterranean herbs in terra-cotta pots. They make beautiful table displays and the leaves can be used in myriad recipes.

Speckled quail eggs, home-dyed hens' eggs and globes of bay leaves connote Easter's earthly splendors. To make the herb globes, attach bay laurel or other leaves to a Styrofoam ball with a hot-glue gun. If desired, gird each sphere with wire for extra holding.

ASPARAGUS & POTATOES WITH ALMONDS & MINT

SERVES 6

In this quickly assembled vegetable combination, pine nuts would also go well with the mint and fresh basil with the almonds.

24 small new red potatoes (about 3 lb/ 1.5 kg)
about 2 tablespoons olive oil for coating plus ¼ cup (2 fl oz/60 ml)
salt and freshly ground pepper to taste
2 lb (1 kg) fresh asparagus
1 cup (8 fl oz/250 ml) chicken stock
2 cloves garlic, minced
½ cup (2 oz/60 g) toasted sliced or slivered almonds (see glossary)
½ cup (¾ oz/20 g) chopped fresh mint or basil

Preheat an oven to 400°F (200°C). Place the potatoes in a baking pan, coat them with about 2 tablespoons of the olive oil and sprinkle with salt and pepper. Roast until the potatoes are cooked through but firm, about 25–35 minutes depending on size. Remove from the oven and let sit until cool enough to handle.

❧ Meanwhile, prepare the asparagus. Snap off the tough end of each stalk. If the stalks are thick, peel the bottom 2–3 inches (5–7.5 cm) with a vegetable peeler. Bring about 2 inches (5 cm) of salted water to a boil in a frying pan. Lay the asparagus in the pan and cook until tender-crisp, 3–5 minutes. Remove the asparagus and plunge them into ice water, then drain and pat dry. Cut the asparagus into 2-inch (5-cm) lengths.

❧ Cut the cooled potatoes into quarters. Warm the ¼ cup (2 fl oz/60 ml) olive oil in a very large sauté pan. Add the potatoes and heat them through. Add the asparagus, chicken stock and garlic and simmer a few minutes to heat through. Season with salt and pepper, then add the almonds and mint or basil and serve.

Asparagus & Potatoes with Almonds & Mint

CITRUS & HONEY CHEESECAKE WITH NUT CRUST

MAKES ONE 9-INCH (23-CM) CHEESECAKE

Use dark honey for a fuller-bodied, more intense flavor. The cheesecake is best served slightly warm or at room temperature.

FOR THE CRUST:

2 cups (8 oz/250 g) hazelnuts, toasted and skinned (see glossary)

⅓ cup (3 oz/90 g) sugar

½ teaspoon ground cinnamon

4–5 tablespoons (2–2½ oz/60–80 g) unsalted butter, melted

FOR THE CHEESE FILLING:

1½ lb (750 g) cream cheese at room temperature

½ cup (4 fl oz/125 ml) sour cream at room temperature

¾ cup (9 oz/280 g) full-flavored honey

6 eggs, separated, at room temperature

1 tablespoon grated lemon zest

1 tablespoon grated orange zest

1 teaspoon vanilla extract (essence)

3 tablespoons chopped candied orange peel, optional

¼ cup (2 oz/60 g) sugar

FOR THE GARNISH:

chopped toasted and skinned hazelnuts (see glossary)

fresh strawberries, optional

Citrus & Honey Cheesecake with Nut Crust

To make the crust, chop the nuts with the sugar and cinnamon in a food processor as finely as possible; do not let it turn to paste. Add enough butter for the mixture to hold together. Press this mixture into the bottom and partially up the sides of a 9-inch (23-cm) spring-form pan. Set aside.

❧ To make the filling, preheat an oven to 350°F (180°C). Place the cream cheese and sour cream in the bowl of an electric mixer. Beat until smooth with the paddle attachment or beaters. Add the honey and beat until there are no lumps. Add the egg yolks, lemon and orange zests, vanilla and, if using, candied orange peel; mix well.

❧ In a large bowl, beat the egg whites until frothy. Gradually beat in the sugar until the peaks are almost stiff. Stir one third of the egg whites into the cheese mixture, then fold in the rest. Pour into the prepared cake pan. Bake on the middle rack of the oven until set just on the edges, about 45–50 minutes; gently shake the pan to test. Turn off the oven and leave the cheesecake inside with the door ajar for 2 hours.

❧ Remove the sides from the pan and slide the cheesecake onto a plate. Top with chopped hazelnuts and, if desired, arrange berries around the cheesecake.

TRADITIONAL THANKSGIVING

American families everywhere hold the national harvest celebration dear to their hearts. The Thanksgiving feast has provided many enduring holiday memories and features a roster of ingredients so ritualized that they have become almost sacred.

We presented our Thanksgiving menu in a classic American dining room featuring an extra-long table so it could accommodate not only the guests but also the roast turkey. Side dishes and other courses were placed close at hand on a sideboard. We also set up a separate children's table, a tradition in some families. Heirloom dishes and antique silver, glassware and linens were selected to reinforce a sense of family heritage. Wheat sheaves, baskets, nuts, and game-bird feathers helped to evoke the spirit of the American harvest.

Menu

Spiced Squash & Apple Soup

---

*Roast Turkey with
Corn Bread Stuffing*

Cranberry Chutney

*Chanterelles, Chestnuts &
Pearl Onions with Thyme*

Celery Root & Potato Purée

*Brussels Sprouts
with Garlic & Parmesan*

Tangerine Custard Tart

As our holiday menu shows, there is room for creativity within the traditional bounds of the Thanksgiving meal. Here butternut squash takes over for pumpkin in the first-course soup, while a vivid tangerine custard assumes the pumpkin's usual role as a pie filling. The turkey features a corn bread stuffing enriched with sweet Italian sausage, and subtle spices perfume the cranberry sauce.

It takes advance planning to cook and serve such an extensive menu. We recommend that you carefully read through the preparation list and the recipes up to several weeks before Thanksgiving Day, allowing yourself ample time for shopping and advance cooking. Mix and match this menu with your own favorites as you wish.

WINE RECOMMENDATIONS

The first choice to accompany Thanksgiving turkey is a just-released Beaujolais Nouveau. For white wine drinkers, pour a Riesling from the Rhine or Mosel regions of Germany. With dessert, offer a late-harvest Semillon from Australia or America, or an outstanding Sauternes.

Keep place settings simple. Set the soup plate atop the dinner plate and provide only essential cutlery and glasses. Left, baskets and bowls of nuts, and dried Native American corn are strong symbols of Thanksgiving's blessings.

PREPARATION LIST

• Up to 1 week ahead, make the chutney.

• Up to 2 days ahead, make and refrigerate the tangerine custard pie filling.

• The day before, make the soup; prepare the stuffing (but do not stuff the turkey).

• On Thanksgiving morning, prepare and bake the pie crust.

• Three hours before, fill and top the pie.

• Up to several hours ahead, prepare the celery root and potato purée.

• Fifteen minutes before, bake the chanterelle casserole; start cooking the Brussels sprouts.

EACH RECIPE YIELDS 12 SERVINGS

A wooden cupboard opens to reveal a collection of glistening Early American silver pieces for coffee and tea service.

SPICED SQUASH & APPLE SOUP

SERVES 12

Butternut squash is similar to pumpkin in taste and texture but is easier to peel and dice. Apple lightens and sweetens the purée.

4 tablespoons (2 oz/60 g) unsalted
   butter or olive oil
2 large onions, diced, about 4 cups
   (1¼ lb/625 g)
2 large green apples, peeled, cored and
   diced, about 2 cups (1 lb/500 g)
1 teaspoon ground nutmeg
½ teaspoon ground allspice
½ teaspoon ground cinnamon
10 cups (5 lb/2.4 kg) peeled and diced
   butternut squash (about 4 whole)
12 cups (3 qt/3 l) chicken stock
salt and freshly ground pepper to taste
thin slices of green apple for garnish

*M*elt the butter or heat the olive oil in a large pot over moderate heat. Add the diced onions and apples and cook until tender, about 10 minutes. Stir in the spices, cook for 1 minute, then add the squash and chicken stock. Bring to a boil, reduce the heat and simmer, uncovered, until the squash is very tender, about 20–30 minutes.

ᐸᙥ Purée the vegetables in batches with a little bit of the stock in a blender or food processor. Transfer to a large bowl. Add enough of the remaining stock to make a medium-thick soup. Reserve any leftover stock if not serving right away, as the soup may thicken on standing. Season with salt and pepper and adjust the spices. This soup may be made a day ahead, refrigerated uncovered until cold and then covered.

ᐸᙥ To serve, in a large pot heat the soup almost to scalding. Ladle into bowls and top with thin slices of apple.

*A*long with the soup, serve basketfuls of bakery breads. Loaves with raised decorations in the forms of wheat, hearts and leaves are especially homey.

Spiced Squash & Apple Soup

ROAST TURKEY WITH CORN BREAD STUFFING

SERVES 12

While the turkey roasts, make the giblet stock; just before carving, use the stock to make the gravy. For best results, always use fresh (not frozen) turkey.

FOR THE STUFFING:
2 tablespoons olive oil
1 lb (500 g) sweet Italian sausages, removed from casings and crumbled
6 tablespoons (3 oz/90 g) unsalted butter
2 onions, diced, about 1½ cups (8 oz/250 g)
1 cup (5 oz/155 g) diced celery
2 cloves garlic, minced
2 tablespoons finely chopped fresh marjoram or sage
2 teaspoons ground fennel seed
½ teaspoon ground nutmeg
½ teaspoon ground cinnamon
1 cup (8 fl oz/250 ml) chicken stock
4 cups (8 oz/250 g) packaged corn bread stuffing
salt and freshly ground pepper to taste

FOR THE TURKEY:
1 fresh turkey, 12–14 lb (6–7 kg), neck and giblets removed for gravy
1 lemon, cut in half
1 clove garlic
salt, freshly ground pepper and sweet paprika to taste

FOR THE GIBLET STOCK AND GRAVY:
turkey neck and giblets
8 cups (64 fl oz/2 l) water or chicken stock
2 sliced onions
2 sliced peeled carrots
1 or 2 celery ribs
1 fresh thyme sprig
1 clove garlic
2 tablespoons all-purpose (plain) flour
salt, freshly ground pepper and ground allspice to taste

To prepare the stuffing, heat the oil in a large sauté pan. Add the sausage and sauté until browned. Remove from the pan with a slotted spoon and set aside. Add the butter to the pan and cook the onions until translucent, about 10 minutes. Add the celery, garlic, marjoram or sage, fennel seed, nutmeg, cinnamon and the stock and cook 3 minutes longer. Transfer to a large bowl and add the sausage and corn bread. Season with salt and pepper and mix well. At this point, you can cover and refrigerate the stuffing overnight.

❧ To prepare the turkey, preheat an oven to 350°F (180°C). Wipe the turkey with a damp cloth and rub the body cavity with the cut lemon and garlic and salt. Sprinkle the outside with salt, pepper and paprika.

❧ Spoon the stuffing loosely into the body and neck cavities and sew or truss them closed. Place any extra stuffing in a buttered casserole, moisten with a little extra stock and cover. Place in the oven 1 hour before the turkey is done.

❧ To roast the turkey, place it breast-side down on a rack in a roasting pan. Tent with aluminum foil. Roast for 20 minutes per pound (4–4½ hours total). Uncover the turkey and turn it breast-side up for the last 45 minutes of baking.

❧ Meanwhile, to prepare the giblet stock, simmer the neck, gizzard and heart (do not use the liver) in a large pan with the water or stock, onions, carrots, celery, thyme and garlic. Bring to a boil, then reduce heat and simmer for 1½ hours, skimming the surface; add more stock as needed. Remove the neck and discard. Remove the giblets and chop fine. Discard the thyme. Transfer the cooked vegetables with a slotted spoon to a blender and purée. Reserve the giblets, giblet stock and the puréed vegetables to make the gravy.

❧ The turkey is done when a meat thermometer inserted in the thickest part of the thigh (away from the bone) registers 180°F (82°C). Remove from the oven and let rest at least 15 minutes before carving. Remove the stuffing.

❧ To make the gravy, pour off all but 3 tablespoons of drippings from the roasting pan. Place the pan over medium heat and stir in the 2 tablespoons flour until bubbly, then add 1 cup (8 fl oz/250 ml) of the reserved giblet stock. Bring to a boil. Stir in the vegetable purée and thin with additional stock. Add the chopped giblets. Season with salt, pepper and allspice. Carve the turkey (see page 178). Serve with the stuffing and gravy.

CRANBERRY CHUTNEY

MAKES ABOUT 6 CUPS (48 OZ/1.5 KG)

This sweetly spiced variation on traditional cranberry sauce may be made weeks ahead.

2 cups (16 fl oz/500 ml) water
3 cups (1½ lb/750 g) sugar
2 unpeeled oranges, diced, seeded and finely chopped in a blender
two 2-inch (5-cm) pieces fresh ginger, peeled and cut into thin slices
4 cups (1 lb/500 g) cranberries
1 teaspoon ground cinnamon
½ teaspoon ground cloves
1 cup (6 oz/185 g) raisins

*C*ombine the water and sugar in a deep saucepan and bring to a boil, stirring. Add the oranges and ginger; reduce heat and simmer, uncovered, for 20 minutes. Add the cranberries, cinnamon and cloves and cook, uncovered, until thickened, about 15 minutes. Stir in the raisins and cook until big bubbles appear, about 7 minutes. Pour into a bowl and let cool. Serve or cover and refrigerate for up to 1 week.

Roast Turkey with Corn Bread Stuffing; Cranberry Chutney

CHANTERELLES, CHESTNUTS & PEARL ONIONS WITH THYME

SERVES 12

Peeling fresh chestnuts is a painstaking task, but worth every minute of hot-fingered torture. See if you can talk someone into helping you, as the chestnuts must be hot for the inner skin to come off. Or purchase canned peeled chestnuts instead.

1 lb (500 g) chestnuts
1 lb (500 g) cipolline or pearl onions
2 lb (1 kg) chanterelles or brown
   mushrooms
8 tablespoons (4 oz/125 g) unsalted
   butter
2 tablespoons chopped fresh thyme
½ cup (4 fl oz/125 ml) chicken stock,
   or as needed
salt and freshly ground pepper to taste

Cut a cross in the rounded side of each chestnut. Place in a single layer in one or more large saucepans, cover with water and bring to a boil. Reduce heat and simmer, uncovered, for 10 minutes. While the chestnuts are hot, remove the outer peel and the thin inner brown skin. Try to keep the chestnuts whole, if possible. If the center is whiter than the outside, the chestnuts are not cooked through; simmer them in additional water for about 8–10 minutes more. (The chestnuts are done when the inside is the same color as the cooked outer parts. Cut one in half to check.) Set the cooked chestnuts aside.

❧ Trim the roots of the onions carefully without cutting across the ends. Cut a cross on the bottom of each onion to prevent them from telescoping while cooking. Place the onions in a medium saucepan, cover with water and bring to a boil. Reduce heat and sim-

mer, uncovered, until tender-firm, about 8–10 minutes. Drain, let cool slightly, then remove the peels. Set the onions aside.

❧ Wipe the mushrooms clean with a damp paper towel or clean with a mushroom brush. Cut into thick slices. Or, if the mushrooms are small, leave them whole. Melt half of the butter in a large sauté pan and sauté half of the mushrooms over high heat until softened, 3–5 minutes. Repeat with the remaining butter and mushrooms.

❧ To serve, preheat an oven to 350°F (180°C). Combine the cooked chestnuts, onions and mushrooms in a large casserole. Toss with the thyme. Add enough chicken stock to moisten the mixture. Season with salt and pepper. Bake until heated through, about 15 minutes. Serve at once.

CELERY ROOT & POTATO PURÉE

SERVES 12

Celery root contributes a subtle edge of sweetness and lightness. It's best to purée the potatoes with a ricer or food mill since processors yield gummy results.

8 large baking potatoes
3 large celeriacs (celery roots)
3–4 cups (24–32 fl oz/750 ml–1 l)
   chicken stock
6 tablespoons (3 oz/90 g) unsalted butter
1 cup (8 fl oz/250 ml) heavy
   (double) cream
salt, freshly ground pepper and ground
   nutmeg to taste

Preheat an oven to 400°F (200°C). Poke the potatoes in several places with a fork and bake until very tender, about 1 hour. Cut in half, remove the pulp and pass it through a ricer or food mill.

❧ While the potatoes are baking, trim the leaves and roots from the celeriacs and peel. Cut into dice and simmer, uncovered, in enough chicken stock to cover until very tender, about 25 minutes. Drain and purée in a food processor or pass through a food mill.

❧ Combine the potato and celeriac purée in a large, heavy saucepan over moderate heat. Stir in the butter and cream; if necessary add more butter and cream or stock until a thick, smooth consistency is achieved. Season with salt, pepper and a little nutmeg.

BRUSSELS SPROUTS WITH GARLIC & PARMESAN

SERVES 12

The sprouts stand up well to the large quantity of garlic in this vivid green, quickly cooked side dish.

3 lb (1.5 kg) Brussels sprouts
¼ cup (2 oz/60 g) unsalted butter
¼ cup (2 fl oz/60 ml) olive oil
12 large cloves garlic, minced
1½–2 cups (12–16 fl oz/375–500 ml)
   chicken stock
salt and freshly ground pepper to taste
1½ cups (6 oz/185 g) freshly grated
   Parmesan cheese

Trim the ends from the Brussels sprouts and cut the sprouts in half lengthwise. Heat the butter and oil in 1 or 2 sauté pans large enough to hold all the Brussels sprouts in one layer. Add the garlic and cook over low heat to remove the bite, about 2 minutes. Add the Brussels sprouts and chicken stock to a depth of 1½ inches (4 cm) and cover the pan. Simmer until tender-crisp, stirring occasionally, about 5–8 minutes. Season with salt and pepper and top with the cheese. Serve at once.

Brussels Sprouts with Garlic & Parmesan; Celery Root & Potato Purée; Chanterelles, Chestnuts & Pearl Onions with Thyme

TANGERINE CUSTARD TART

MAKES TWO 10-INCH (25-CM) TARTS

*Sweet-tart tangerines make an elegant
curdlike filling for a festive dessert. Be sure
to grate the tangerine zest for the topping
before you juice the fruit for the filling.*

FOR THE TARTS:

12 egg yolks

1 cup (8 fl oz/250 ml) fresh
    tangerine juice

½ cup (4 fl oz/125 ml) fresh
    lemon juice

1½ cups (12 oz/375 g) granulated
    sugar

8 tablespoons (4 oz/125 g) unsalted
    butter, cut into small bits

grated zest of 6 tangerines

2 tablespoons mandarin orange liqueur

basic pie pastry for a double-crust pie
    shell (recipe on page 177)

FOR THE TOPPING:

2 cups (16 fl oz/500 ml) heavy
    (double) cream

¼ cup (1½ oz/45 g) sifted confec-
    tioners' (icing) sugar

grated zest of 4 tangerines

mandarin orange liqueur to taste

To make the filling, combine the egg
yolks, juices and sugar in a bowl. Strain
into a heavy stainless-steel saucepan or
the top part of a double boiler set over,
but not touching, simmering water and
whisk the mixture constantly until
thick. Stir in the butter, zest and mandarin orange liqueur. Cover and chill
for at least 3 hours or up to 2 days.

☙ Roll out half of the pastry and use it
to line a 10-inch (25-cm) tart pan.
Repeat with the other half of the
pastry. Set the shells aside in the freezer
for 30 minutes. Fully bake the pie shells
as directed on page 177. Cool completely, then spread equal amounts of
tangerine filling in each pie shell.

☙ To make the topping, in a bowl
whip the cream until it holds soft peaks;
beat in the confectioners' sugar, tangerine zest and mandarin orange liqueur.
Spread the cream evenly over the top
of each pie, filling almost to the edges.

*Decorate the dessert table with
fresh tangerines arranged with poetic
simplicity in a wooden bowl.*

Tangerine Custard Tart

CASUAL HANUKKAH BUFFET

Hanukkah, the festival of lights, commemorates the rededication of the Temple of Jerusalem some 2,100 years ago. For eight successive evenings in November or December, Jewish families light candles to mark that event. Especially on the first and last nights, they gather together to feast and give gifts.

Appropriate for any convivial get-together in late autumn or winter, our Hanukkah party takes place in a large kitchen, where everyone can savor the warmth and rich aromas. If your kitchen is big enough, by all means use it; at the very least, you can set dishes out on the counter for buffet-style service. We lit candles in a traditional Jewish menorah to mark the start of the meal, but any candlelight will add to the ambience. Displays of fruits and nuts are apt decorations to grace the entire kitchen.

Menu

Beet, Cabbage & Mushroom Borscht

———

Potato Latkes

Chunky Applesauce

Spiced Brisket of Beef

Carrot Tsimmes

———

Pecan Torte

Tangerine Sorbet

This hearty winter buffet is made up of traditional Eastern European–style dishes that have become as synonymous with Hanukkah as turkey is with Thanksgiving. They belong to the category of comfort foods, excellent for any cold-weather meal.

In observation of Jewish dietary laws, we kept the menu free of dairy ingredients. But if you don't keep kosher, feel free to top the borscht and latkes with sour cream and the pecan torte with whipped cream.

Once the candles have been lit, you could start the meal by ladling the soup at the table, then ask guests to join you in the kitchen to cook the latkes. Let guests help themselves from the buffet for the main course and dessert.

WINE RECOMMENDATIONS

Many high-quality kosher wines are made today in Israel, France, New York and California. Select a single red wine for the meal, one which is light to medium in body and both spicy and earthy in flavor: a supple Cabernet Sauvignon or an herbal Merlot would work well. With dessert, sip a tawny port or a cream sherry.

Everyday items, such as baskets, dried wildflowers and decorative containers, adorn a display shelf. Left, the menorah displays one lighted candle for each night of Hanukkah and an additional candle to light the others.

PREPARATION LIST

- Two to 3 days ahead, coat the brisket with the spices.
- Up to 2 days ahead, make and refrigerate the applesauce to be rewarmed before serving.
- The day before, prepare the borscht and make and freeze the sorbet.
- The morning of the party, make the torte.
- Just before dinner, start the potato latkes.

EACH RECIPE YIELDS 12 SERVINGS

Potted narcissus, a simple basket of pears and softly glowing candles symbolize the winter season in a dramatic still-life composition.

BEET, CABBAGE & MUSHROOM BORSCHT

SERVES 12

An Eastern European favorite, this tastes best if made the day before. Supplement any leftovers with extra brisket for the next day's meal.

8–10 large beets (beetroots)
3 tablespoons olive oil
2 large red (Spanish) onions, chopped
6 large carrots, peeled and sliced
2 heads cabbage, shredded
4 cups (12 oz/375 g) sliced
  fresh mushrooms
1 lemon, pricked with a fork in
  several places
10 cups (2½ qt/2.5 l) beef or
  vegetable stock
salt and freshly ground pepper to taste
sugar to taste
fresh lemon juice if needed
½ cup (¾ oz/20 g) chopped
  fresh dill

Cut the greens from the beets, leaving about 2 inches (5 cm) of stems attached. Wash the beets well, place them in a pot and cover with cold water. Bring to a boil, then reduce the heat and simmer, uncovered, until tender, about 30–50 minutes, depending on the size of the beets. Drain. Cover the beets with lukewarm water. When cool, slip off the skins and dice the beets. Set aside.

In a stockpot, warm the olive oil over moderate heat. Add the onions and carrots and cook for about 10 minutes, stirring occasionally. Add the cabbage, beets, mushrooms, lemon and stock; bring to a boil. Reduce the heat and simmer, uncovered, until the soup is red and the flavors are blended, about 30 minutes. Remove the lemon. Season with salt and pepper; adjust the seasoning with sugar and lemon juice if necessary. Sprinkle with chopped dill before serving.

Beet, Cabbage & Mushroom Borscht

POTATO LATKES

MAKES ABOUT 24 POTATO PANCAKES

Grate the potatoes and onions for more robust potato pancakes; dice and purée them for finer-textured results.

2 small onions
6–7 large russet potatoes, peeled
2 large eggs, beaten
2 teaspoons salt
1 teaspoon freshly ground pepper
¾–1 cup (4–5 oz/125–155 g)
   all-purpose (plain) flour
vegetable shortening or oil for frying

Grate the onions and potatoes and place them in a large bowl. Using paper towels, blot up any liquid they might have released and stir in the eggs, salt, pepper and enough flour to bind the mixture.

❧ Heat 2 inches (5 cm) of melted shortening or oil in a large frying pan and drop in spoonfuls of batter. Cook until golden brown, about 3 minutes on each side. Drain on paper towels and keep warm in a 350°F (180°C) oven while cooking the remaining batter. Serve as soon as the last batch is cooked; latkes will stay crisp for only a few minutes.

❧ Alternately, dice the onions and potatoes. Place half of the diced onions and 1 egg in the container of a blender. Purée until liquified. Add half of the diced potatoes and purée until smooth, but not liquified. Transfer the mixture to a bowl. Repeat with the remaining onions, egg and potatoes. Combine the 2 batches in a bowl, add the salt and pepper and blot up any excess liquid with paper towels. Fold in the flour. Cook as directed above.

Potato Latkes; Chunky Applesauce

CHUNKY APPLESAUCE

MAKES 4–5 CUPS (32–40 FL OZ/1–1.2 L)

A traditional companion to potato latkes, this applesauce has a bracing tartness. If you wish, add a little more sugar to taste.

8–10 apples, peeled, cored and cut into
   1-inch (2.5-cm) chunks
juice of 2–3 oranges, about 1 cup
   (8 fl oz/250 ml)
½ cup (4 oz/125 g) sugar or to taste
2 teaspoons grated lemon zest
½ teaspoon ground cinnamon

Place the apples and orange juice in a heavy sauté pan. Cook over moderate heat, stirring often, until the apples start to soften, about 10 minutes. Stir in the sugar, lemon zest and cinnamon and cook, uncovered, until tender but still chunky, about 20–25 minutes. Adjust the seasoning and serve warm. Or cool, cover and refrigerate for up to 2 days. Rewarm before serving.

SPICED BRISKET OF BEEF

SERVES 12

A blend of Middle Eastern spices adds an exotic touch to the classic Jewish braised brisket.

1 brisket of beef, about 10 lb (5 kg)
½ cup (4 oz/125 g) sugar
1 teaspoon ground nutmeg
1 teaspoon ground cloves
1 teaspoon ground allspice
2 tablespoons ground pepper
1 teaspoon ground ginger
6 tablespoons (3 fl oz/90 ml) olive oil or chicken fat
salt to taste
12 cups (3 lb/1.5 kg) diced onions
2 cups (16 fl oz/500 ml) beef stock or as needed
2 cups (16 fl oz/500 ml) tomato purée (see glossary)

Place the meat in a large glass or plastic container. Combine the sugar, nutmeg, cloves, allspice, pepper and ginger and sprinkle them over the meat. Cover and refrigerate for 2 days, turning once each day. Lift the meat from the marinade and pat dry.

❧ Heat 3 tablespoons of the oil or fat in a large heavy frying pan or on a griddle. Sprinkle the meat with salt and brown on both sides. Set aside.

❧ In a heavy pot large enough to hold the brisket, heat the remaining 3 tablespoons oil or fat and cook the onions until tender and translucent, about 10 minutes. Place the beef atop the onions and cover the pot. Reduce the heat and simmer the brisket for 2 hours. Add the beef stock if the onions and beef haven't exuded enough juices;

Spiced Brisket of Beef; Carrot Tsimmes

you will need about 3 cups (24 fl oz/ 750 ml) of liquid. Add the tomato purée and cook until the meat is tender, about 1 hour longer.

❧ Remove the brisket to a carving board and let rest, covered with aluminum foil, for 10 minutes. Cook the pan juices over medium heat to reduce them if they are too thin or lack flavor. Adjust the seasoning. Slice the meat across the grain and serve with the pan juices.

CARROT TSIMMES

SERVES 12

In Yiddish, the term tsimmes *often describes a messy situation. Add sweet potatoes or dried fruit, if you like, to this flavorful mess.*

1 cup (6 oz/185 g) raisins
3 tablespoons vegetable oil or chicken fat
2 onions, sliced thin
24 carrots, peeled and cut into ¼-inch (6-mm) slices
6 tablespoons (4 oz/125 g) honey
grated zest of 2 lemons
chicken stock or wine
salt and freshly ground pepper to taste

Soak the raisins in hot water to cover for 10 minutes; drain, reserving the raisin water to use in the tsimmes.

❧ Heat the oil or fat in a large saucepan. Add the sliced onions and cook until tender, about 5 minutes. Add the carrots, honey, lemon zest, raisin water and enough stock or wine to cover the carrots. Bring to a boil, reduce heat, cover and simmer until the carrots are tender, about 10–15 minutes. You may need to add a bit more liquid from time to time. Add the raisins in the last 5 minutes. Season with salt and pepper.

Foil-wrapped chocolate coins, known as gelt, are a traditional Hanukkah party favor. Usually given to the children as tokens of prosperity and goodwill, you can set the coins out in a small basket or a net bag, or strew them festively around the table.

If your plan for this Hanukkah Buffet includes giving a small gift, homemade preserves are a loving reminder of the fruits of your kitchen. Dress each jar with an illustrated label showing the fruit used in the preserve, if possible. A soft-colored ribbon is all the wrapping you need. Of course, top-quality purchased jams are a delicious present as well.

PECAN TORTE

MAKES ONE 10-INCH (25-CM) TORTE

The torte includes tangerine zest to link it to its accompanying sorbet. At a non-kosher meal, top it with whipped cream.

3 cups (12 oz/375 g) chopped pecans
1½ cups (12 oz/375 g) sugar
10 eggs, separated
½ cup (4 fl oz/125 ml) fresh
   tangerine juice
grated zest of 3 tangerines
½ cup (2 oz/60 g) sifted all-purpose
   (plain) flour
½ teaspoon salt
1 teaspoon ground cinnamon
chopped candied tangerine peel,
   optional

Preheat an oven to 350°F (180°C). Oil and flour a 10-inch (25-cm) tube pan or angel food cake pan and set aside.
❧ Chop the nuts with ½ cup (4 oz/ 125 g) of the sugar in a food processor as finely as possible; do not let it turn to paste. Set aside.
❧ In the bowl of an electric mixer, combine the egg yolks and ½ cup (4 oz/ 125 g) of the remaining sugar, set the bowl over hot water and whisk for a few minutes until warm. Remove from the hot water and beat on high speed with the whisk attachment until the mixture is very thick and pale and a small amount trailed from the whisk forms a ribbon on the surface of the mixture, about 8 minutes. Stir in the tangerine juice and zest.
❧ In a bowl, toss the nut mixture with the flour, salt and cinnamon, then gradually fold these dry ingredients into the yolks with a rubber spatula.
❧ In a large bowl, beat the egg whites until soft peaks form. Gradually beat in the remaining ½ cup (4 oz/125 g) sugar. Fold the whites into the batter. Fold in the optional candied peel. Pour the batter into the prepared pan and bake until a toothpick inserted in the center of the cake comes out clean, about 45 minutes. Let cool in the pan, then invert onto a plate; slice to serve.

TANGERINE SORBET

MAKES ABOUT 4 CUPS (32 FL OZ/1 L)

Whole tangerines, at their peak during the holidays, are traditionally given as gifts to children at the Hanukkah feast. Be sure to grate the zest before juicing the fruit.

4 cups (32 fl oz/1 l) fresh tangerine juice
1½ cups (12 oz/375 g) sugar
1 tablespoon fresh lemon juice
2 tablespoons grated tangerine zest

Combine 2 cups (16 fl oz/500 ml) of the tangerine juice and the sugar in small saucepan. Cook, stirring occasionally, until the sugar dissolves and the mixture is clear. Set aside and let cool. Stir in the remaining tangerine juice and lemon juice. Add the zest. Freeze in an ice cream maker according to the manufacturer's instructions.

Pecan Torte; Tangerine Sorbet

CHRISTMAS SEASON OPEN HOUSE

At no other time of year are we more likely to invite friends and family to drop by than during the month of December. Holiday gatherings, whether for traditional gift exchanges or simply to share good cheer, call for a menu that can be prepared in advance and served buffet-style.

Our Christmas season open house takes place in a living room, where guests can comfortably mingle around the tree and beside the hearth. Traditional ornaments play the major role in setting the party's scene. You'll probably want to supplement yours with an abundance of seasonal touches; pinecones, boughs of holly and sprigs of mistletoe, wreaths of various sizes and myriad glowing candles fill the room with warmth and merriment. If you have a fireplace and the weather is cold, keep the flames roaring all day long.

Menu

Savory Biscotti

Herbed Cheese Spread

Country Pâté

———

Potato & Onion Pizza

Mushroom Blintzes

Duck with Lentils

———

Chestnut Torte with
Chocolate Mocha Butter Cream

This Christmas buffet menu for eighteen is as robust and warming as the season itself. There are light dishes for guests who just want to nibble, as well as hearty recipes for those who want a complete meal.

To arrange separate stations for serving the different dishes, clear coffee tables, side tables and other surfaces in a living room, dining room or den. Present the biscotti, cheese and pâté arranged on platters to welcome newcomers. Replenish the pizza, blintzes and duck hot from the oven as the afternoon or evening progresses. A variety of other beverages, including a favorite hot cider or cocoa, may be served as well as the wine.

WINE RECOMMENDATIONS

Offer both white and red. For the white, try a medium-to-full-bodied, assertive wine with notes of spice and earth: a rustic Pinot Blanc or a flinty Chardonnay. For the red, select an Australian Shiraz or a simple French country wine such as Madiran or Corbières. With dessert, offer a Malmsey Madeira or a brown or cream sherry from Spain.

An ensemble of natural decorations, including pinecones, oranges, fir boughs and cranberries, flanks a log birdhouse to create a miniature winter scene. Left, a punch bowl of cider mulled with citrus zests, sugar and sweet spices offers holiday warmth to guests on arrival.

PREPARATION LIST

- Up to 2 weeks ahead, prepare the pâté.

- Up to 2 days ahead, make the biscotti and store them in an airtight container; make and refrigerate the cheese spread.

- The day before, roast and cut up the ducks; make the lentils. Refrigerate them separately.

- The morning of the party, make and refrigerate the crêpes; make and refrigerate the torte.

- Several hours ahead, make the pizza dough and toppings, to be assembled and baked just before serving.

THIS MENU SERVES 18 GUESTS. FOR A SMALLER PARTY, OFFER FEWER DISHES.

Napkins in a plaid pattern of traditional holiday colors are folded as buffet servers (see page 183) to hold knives and forks.

SAVORY BISCOTTI

MAKES 48 BISCOTTI

Make a double batch so you'll have extra throughout the holidays. Recrisp them on a baking sheet in a 350°F (180°C) oven for 5 minutes.

1 cup (8 oz/250 g) unsalted butter at room temperature
1 cup (8 oz/250 g) sugar
6 eggs
2 tablespoons aquavit (see glossary)
4½ cups (1⅓ lb/665 g) all-purpose (plain) flour
2 teaspoons salt
1 tablespoon baking powder
¼ cup (2 oz/60 g) toasted cumin seeds, crushed (see glossary)
3 tablespoons toasted caraway seeds, crushed (see glossary)
2 cups (8 oz/250 g) ground toasted walnuts (see glossary)

Preheat an oven to 350°F (180°C). In a large bowl, beat the butter and sugar until fluffy. Add the eggs and aquavit and beat well. Add the flour, salt, baking powder, cumin seeds, caraway seeds and walnuts and mix until blended. Form into 4 oval logs and place on 2 ungreased baking sheets. Bake until golden brown and firm to the touch, about 30 minutes. Remove from the oven and let cool on a rack for about 10 minutes.

෴ Reduce the oven temperature to 250°F (120°C). Cut the logs diagonally into ½-inch (12-mm) slices and lay the slices flat on the baking sheets. Bake until dried, about 8–10 minutes longer. Let cool, then store in an airtight container for up to 2 days, or freeze for longer storage.

HERBED CHEESE SPREAD

MAKES ABOUT 5 CUPS (40 OZ/1.25 KG)

Influenced by Italian, French and Romanian dishes, this creamy spread is also good on pumpernickel bread with watercress and cucumber. It can be made up to 2 days in advance.

3 tablespoons olive oil or unsalted butter
1 tablespoon minced garlic
3 cups (15 oz/470 g) crumbled mild fresh goat cheese or feta cheese
1–2 cups (8–16 oz/250–500 g) ricotta
¼ cup (⅜ oz/10 g) chopped fresh parsley
¼ cup (⅜ oz/10 g) minced fresh chives
2 tablespoons finely chopped fresh thyme
2 teaspoons freshly ground pepper

In a small frying pan, heat the oil or melt the butter over moderate heat, add the garlic and cook until tender but not colored, about 3 minutes. Transfer to a food processor or blender and add the goat or feta cheese, 1 cup of the ricotta, the parsley, chives, thyme and pepper. Process to combine. Taste and add more ricotta if goat cheese flavor is too strong. Transfer to a small crock or serving dish. Cover and refrigerate until serving time.

Everybody loves crunchy fresh vegetables, especially when served along with rich holiday fare. Present spears of cucumbers and carrots, endive leaves, crisp scallions and cherry tomatoes near the biscotti and herbed cheese spread for guests to snack on. Use double old-fashioned glasses or French confiture jars to hold each kind of crudité upright.

Savory Biscotti; Herbed Cheese Spread

COUNTRY PÂTÉ

MAKES THREE 9- BY 5- BY 3-INCH
(23- BY 13- BY 7.5-CM) PÂTÉS

Weighting is essential to compact these pâtés. Use another loaf pan or a flat object that fits inside the rim, topped with kitchen weights, heavy cans or bricks. Children's building blocks work in a pinch, too.

1 lb (500 g) finely ground veal
2 lb (1 kg) finely ground pork shoulder
½ lb (250 g) pork fat, coarsely ground
2 lb (1 kg) chicken livers
¼ cup (2 fl oz/60 ml) heavy
    (double) cream
½ cup (3 oz/90 g) all-purpose
    (plain) flour
3 eggs
½ cup (4 fl oz/125 ml) Cognac
    or Armagnac
8 large cloves garlic
1 teaspoon ground nutmeg
½ teaspoon ground allspice
½ teaspoon ground ginger
½ teaspoon ground cinnamon

Country Pâté

4 teaspoons salt
2 teaspoons freshly ground pepper
9–12 bay leaves
6 thin sheets pork fat (2 combined should
    be large enough to cover each loaf)
3 large baguettes, sliced
cornichon pickles

*P*reheat an oven to 400°F (200°C). Oil three 9- by 5- by 3-inch (23- by 13- by 7.5-cm) loaf pans and set aside. Combine the ground veal, ground pork and fat in a large bowl. Combine the livers, cream, flour, eggs, Cognac or Armagnac, garlic, nutmeg, allspice, ginger, cinnamon, salt and pepper in a large food processor (or in a blender, in batches) and purée. Combine with the ground meat and mix until well blended.
❧ Pour the mixture into the prepared loaf pans. Top each loaf with a few bay leaves and 2 sheets of fat cut to fit the pan. Cover the loaf pans with a double thickness of aluminum foil. Place the loaf pans in a large baking pan and add hot water to come halfway up the sides.

❧ Bake for 2 hours. Remove and reserve the aluminum foil. Continue baking until lightly browned, about 20 minutes longer. Remove from the oven and re-cover with the foil. Place another loaf pan on top of each pâté and weight it with heavy tins. Let the pâtés sit until cool. Chill well. These pâtés will keep for about 2 weeks under refrigeration. To serve, unmold the pâtés, slice and offer with baguettes and cornichons.

POTATO & ONION PIZZA

SERVES 18

Instead of mixing prosciutto strips with the onions, thin slices of the ham may be draped over the pizza after baking.

FOR THE CRUST:

1 tablespoon active dry yeast
1¼ cups (10 fl oz/300 ml) warm
    (110°F/43°C) water
3½ cups (1⅛ lb/560 g) unbleached
    all-purpose (plain) flour
⅓ cup (1½ oz/45 g) rye or buckwheat
    flour or an additional ⅓ cup
    (2 oz/60 g) all-purpose (plain) flour
3 tablespoons olive oil
1 teaspoon salt
3 tablespoons finely chopped
    fresh rosemary

FOR THE TOPPING:

8 small red new potatoes
6 tablespoons (3 fl oz/90 ml) olive oil
salt and freshly ground pepper to taste
4 large onions, sliced thin
1 cup (4 oz/125 g) long, thin prosciutto
    strips, optional
cornmeal for sprinkling
1 tablespoon minced garlic
1–1½ cups (4–6 oz/125–185 g)
    grated mozzarella
2 tablespoons chopped fresh sage
    or rosemary
½ cup (2 oz/60 g) freshly grated Parmesan

Potato & Onion Pizza

To make the crust, dissolve the yeast in ½ cup (4 fl oz/125 ml) of the warm water in the bowl of an electric mixer. Add ½ cup (2½ oz/75 g) of the all-purpose (plain) flour and mix to combine. Cover and let sit for about 30 minutes.

🍃 Add the remaining all-purpose flour, buckwheat flour, remaining water, olive oil, salt and rosemary and mix well. Beat on low speed with the dough hook attached until the dough leaves the sides of the bowl cleanly, about 10 minutes. Or, to make by hand, knead on a lightly floured board for about 10 minutes, or until the dough is no longer sticky. Transfer the dough to an oiled bowl, cover with a towel and let rise in a warm place until doubled, about 1 hour.

🍃 Meanwhile, to make the topping, preheat an oven to 400°F (200°C). Place the potatoes in a small baking pan. Brush the potatoes with 1 tablespoon of the olive oil, sprinkle with salt and pepper and roast for 25–30 minutes, or until cooked through but firm. Let cool, then cut into ¼-inch-thick (6-mm) slices.

🍃 Heat 3 more tablespoons of the oil in a large sauté pan, add the onions and cook, stirring occasionally, until tender and translucent, about 10 minutes. Caramelize the onions by continuing to cook them until golden, if desired. Season with salt and pepper and stir in the prosciutto, if using. Set aside.

🍃 Turn the dough out onto a lightly floured board. Shape into a ball. Cover and allow to rest in the refrigerator for 30 minutes. Meanwhile, preheat an oven to 475°F (240°C).

🍃 Roll and stretch the dough into 1 large rectangle; place on a baking sheet sprinkled with cornmeal. Mix the garlic and the remaining 2 tablespoons oil and spread over the dough. Top with the mozzarella, then with the cooked onions and potatoes. Sprinkle with the chopped sage or rosemary and the Parmesan. Bake until the edges are golden brown and puffed, about 12–15 minutes. Brush the edges of the pizza with additional olive oil to add a shine, if desired.

Mushroom Blintzes

Makes 36 blintzes

In this Russian-inspired dish, thin crêpes, or blini, *are folded around a mushroom filling in neat parcels resembling Jewish deli blintzes.*

For the Crêpes:

1 cup (8 fl oz/250 ml) cold water
1 cup (8 fl oz/250 ml) cold milk
4 eggs
½ teaspoon salt
2 cups (8 oz/250 g) sifted all-purpose (plain) flour
¼ cup (2 oz/60 g) unsalted butter, melted

For the Filling:

8 tablespoons (4 oz/125 g) unsalted butter, plus additional for cooking blintzes
2 cups (10 oz/315 g) finely chopped onions
1½ lb (750 g) fresh mushrooms, chopped coarsely
2 teaspoons minced garlic
4 teaspoons chopped fresh thyme or 5 tablespoons (½ oz/15 g) chopped fresh dill
3–4 tablespoons all-purpose (plain) flour
⅓ cup (3 fl oz/90 ml) Madeira or sherry
½ cup (4 fl oz/125 ml) chicken stock, if needed
salt and freshly ground pepper to taste

To Cook and Serve the Blintzes:

12 tablespoons (6 oz/180 g) unsalted butter
sour cream, optional

To make the crêpes, put the water, milk, eggs and salt in a blender or food processor. Add the flour and melted butter and blend until smooth. Cover and let the batter rest in the refrigerator for about 2 hours.

Lightly butter a small (about 7-in/18-cm) crêpe pan or small nonstick sauté pan and place it over moderate heat. Ladle 2 tablespoons of batter into the pan and swirl it around until it coats the bottom of the pan. Let cook for a minute or two until set and not shiny. Loosen the crêpe with a spatula, then flip it or turn it with both hands and cook for 30 seconds on the other side. Slide the crêpe out of the pan. Repeat until all the batter is used, stacking the cooked crêpes.

To make the filling, melt 3 tablespoons of the butter in a sauté pan over moderate heat and cook the onions until tender and translucent, about 10 minutes. Lift out and set aside. Melt the remaining 5 tablespoons (2½ oz/80 g) butter in the pan as needed and cook the mushrooms in batches over very high heat so they don't give off too much liquid, about 5 minutes. Place all the cooked mushrooms in the pan and add the garlic. Cook for 1 minute, return the onions to the pan, add the thyme or dill and flour and cook for 3 minutes, stirring constantly. Add the Madeira or sherry and cook until the mixture holds together, 3–4 minutes; if too dry, add enough stock to moisten. Season with salt and pepper.

To assemble the blintzes, place 2 generous tablespoons of filling in the center of each crêpe. Tuck in the sides and fold the top over the bottom edge to make a neat packet. Repeat until all the filling is used. Melt about 2 tablespoons of the butter in a sauté pan and fry the blintzes in batches of 6 until golden on both sides. Keep warm, covered with aluminum foil. Repeat, adding the remaining butter as needed, until all the blintzes are cooked. Serve with dollops of sour cream, if desired.

Duck with Lentils

Serves 18

Based on traditional French and Italian winter fare, this recipe extracts more fat from the ducks by roasting instead of braising them. If you have only one small oven, roast the ducks two at a time.

For the Ducks:

6 ducks, about 5 lb (2.5 kg) each, necks and wing tips removed and reserved, and excess fat removed
12 cloves garlic, minced
grated zest of 6 large lemons
2 tablespoons salt
2 tablespoons freshly ground pepper
12 fresh thyme or marjoram sprigs
3 lemons, cut into quarters

For the Lentils:

6 cups (2½ lb/1.25 kg) lentils, preferably French green lentils
14 cups (3½ qt/3.5 l) water
½ cup (4 oz/125 g) unsalted butter
6 large onions, diced, about 6 cups (1½ lb/750 g)
6 large carrots, peeled and cut into ¼-inch (6-mm) dice
3 ribs celery, cut into ¼-inch (6-mm) dice
2 tablespoons minced garlic
1 teaspoon ground cinnamon
2 teaspoons ground cumin
4 Pippin or other tart green apples, peeled, cored and diced
2 cups (16 fl oz/500 ml) chicken stock
½ cup (¾ oz/20 g) chopped fresh parsley
3 tablespoons chopped fresh thyme or marjoram
2 tablespoons grated lemon zest
salt and freshly ground pepper to taste

To prepare the ducks, preheat an oven or ovens to 475°F (240°C). Place 2 ducks on a rack in each of 3 large roasting pans. Prick the ducks evenly all over with a fork. Mash together the garlic, lemon zest, salt and pepper and spread this over the inside and outside of the birds. Place the herbs and lemon quarters inside the ducks. Roast until they are tender and well browned and the juices run clear when the thighs are pierced with a knife, about 1 hour. Let sit until cool enough to handle, then cut the ducks into quarters with shears, cutting off and discarding the backbones. Set aside.

❧ Meanwhile, to make the lentils, combine them with the water in a large pot and bring to a boil. Reduce the heat and simmer, covered, until the lentils are tender but still firm to the bite, about 20 minutes for brown lentils, or up to 25–40 minutes for green lentils. Test them every 5–10 minutes for doneness. Remove from the heat and set aside.

❧ Melt the butter in a large sauté pan with high sides and cook the onions, carrots and celery over moderate heat, stirring occasionally, until they are tender, about 15 minutes. Add the garlic, cinnamon, cumin and apples and cook for 1–2 minutes. Add the lentils and their cooking liquid, stock, herbs and lemon zest; cover and simmer until all the flavors are blended, about 5 minutes. Season to taste with salt and pepper and adjust the spices to taste. The duck and the lentils can be cooked to this point up to 1 day ahead and refrigerated separately.

❧ To serve, combine the duck pieces and lentils in a large heatproof casserole, cover with aluminum foil and place in a preheated 400°F (200°C) oven until bubbly and hot, about 25 minutes.

Mushroom Blintzes; Duck with Lentils

CHESTNUT TORTE WITH CHOCOLATE MOCHA BUTTER CREAM

SERVES 12

Chestnuts, synonymous with winter holidays, combine with a chocolate mocha butter cream for an intensely rich dessert. Look for glacéed chestnuts in specialty food shops or an Italian market.

FOR THE TORTE:
6 large eggs, separated
1½ cups (12 oz/375 g) sugar
1 tablespoon vanilla extract (essence)
2 cups (1 lb/500 g) chestnut purée, pushed through a sieve
1 cup (4 oz/125 g) almonds, finely ground

FOR THE CHOCOLATE MOCHA BUTTER CREAM:
8 oz (250 g) bittersweet chocolate
¼ cup (2 fl oz/60 ml) strong coffee
4 egg yolks
1 cup (8 oz/250 g) sugar
⅓ cup (3 fl oz/90 ml) water
1½ cups (12 oz/375 g) unsalted butter, cut into pieces
3 tablespoons dark rum

FOR THE GARNISH:
whole glacéed chestnuts

Preheat an oven to 350°F (180°C). Butter and flour two 8-inch (20-cm) springform pans.

❧ To prepare the torte, place the egg yolks and 1 cup (8 oz/250 g) of the sugar in the bowl of an electric mixer, set the bowl over hot water and whisk for a few minutes until warm. Remove from the hot water and beat on high speed with the whisk attachment until the mixture is very thick and pale and a small amount trailed from the whisk forms a ribbon on the surface of the mixture, about 8 minutes. Beat in the vanilla, then fold in the chestnut purée and the ground almonds.

❧ Beat the egg whites until soft peaks form, then gradually beat in the remaining ½ cup (4 oz/125 g) sugar until the mixture is stiff but not dry. Stir one third of the whites into the chestnut mixture, then fold in the rest. Divide the batter between the 2 prepared pans and bake until the cakes are pale gold and pull away from the sides of the pans, about 40–50 minutes. Let cool in the pans on racks. Loosen the edges with a knife and then remove the pan sides.

❧ To make the butter cream, combine the chocolate and coffee in the top of a double boiler and melt over simmering water. Set aside and keep warm. Place the egg yolks in the bowl of an electric mixer, set the bowl over hot water and whisk for a few minutes until warm. Remove from the hot water and beat on high speed with the whisk attachment until thick and pale.

❧ Meanwhile, combine the sugar and water in a small saucepan and bring to a boil over high heat, stirring until the sugar dissolves. Boil rapidly until the sugar reaches 236°F (113°C) on a candy thermometer. With the mixer on low speed, gradually beat the hot syrup into the beaten yolks. Fold in the chocolate mixture. Beat in the butter a little at a time. Add the dark rum. Chill until thick enough to spread.

❧ To assemble, place 1 cake on a serving plate, frost it, then place the second cake on top. Frost the top and sides. Refrigerate until the frosting is set, then bring to room temperature for serving. Top with glacéed chestnuts.

Chestnut Torte with Chocolate Mocha Butter Cream

You could have mugs of cocoa and gingerbread men from the bakery on hand as a dessert snack if you are expecting children at your party.

HERITAGE CHRISTMAS DINNER

Most of us lavish more attention on the Yuletide dinner than on any other meal of the year. Whether celebrated on Christmas Eve or Christmas Day, or both, the occasion brings back memories of holidays past and we usually turn faithfully to family traditions when planning the meal.

We set our Christmas dinner in a formal dining room alongside a roaring fire. Rather than conceal the table's beautiful wood surface, we placed an ornate fabric runner down its center; an extra-wide ribbon would work as well.

We decked the mantel and table with wreaths, floral arrangements made up of pine and lilies, silver bowls filled with cranberries and strands of colored beads. The Christmas tree centerpiece is a variation on the easy-to-make Holiday Tree (see page 185). You could make a large one for the main table and smaller ones to go alongside, as shown on these pages.

Menu

Onion Tart

Radicchio, Fennel & Walnut Salad

———

Rib-Eye Roast
with Mustard & Black Pepper

Winter Greens
with Pancetta & Mint

Potato & Sage Gratin

———

Apple Charlotte
with Brandied Whipped Cream
& Apricot Sauce

For Christmas menu inspiration, we looked to the Old World, including dishes from generations past. The recipes that follow reflect a diversity of European cuisines, with an appetizer and dessert from France, an Italian-inspired salad and side dishes, and a traditional English roast beef.

During this busy time of year, careful organization is essential to enjoying the holidays. It's a good idea to begin planning your Christmas dinner at least several weeks in advance by reading through the preparation list and recipes. To ensure that you get the best prime or choice beef roast, order it well ahead of time from a good-quality butcher shop.

WINE RECOMMENDATIONS

Begin with a wine from the Pacific Northwest, such as an Oregon Pinot Gris, or, if you prefer red wine, a Pinot Noir. With the beef, pour an elegant, full-bodied Bordeaux or an aged Rhône such as Châteauneuf-du-Pape. After dessert, pass good-quality Calvados or Cognac.

China accented in gold gleams at a holiday place setting. Fresh cranberries and golden beads placed around the table are a nice accent. Left, achieve lavish results with little effort by attaching gold ornaments to calla lilies and holiday greens.

PREPARATION LIST

• The day before, make the tart crust.

• The morning of the dinner, make the charlotte, to be rewarmed and unmolded before serving.

• Up to 3 hours before dinner, coat the roast with its seasoning spread; prepare the salad ingredients and the dressing.

• Up to 2 hours ahead, assemble the gratin.

• Just before serving, cook the winter greens and toss the salad.

EACH RECIPE YIELDS 6 SERVINGS

Baby pears, lady apples, artichokes and seasonal berries and greens are affixed to an artificial base for this variation on the Holiday Tree (page 185).

The facets of a cut-glass decanter highlight the deep color and clarity of fine red wine poured to accompany the Christmas dinner.

ONION TART

MAKES ONE 9-INCH (23-CM) TART

Serve slices of this classic French quiche as a first course with the radicchio and fennel salad.

basic pie pastry for a single-crust pie
   shell (recipe on page 177)
1½ lb (750 g) large onions
¼ cup (2 oz/60 g) unsalted butter
2 tablespoons oil
salt, freshly ground pepper and ground
   nutmeg to taste
4 eggs
1½ cups (12 fl oz/375 ml) heavy
   (double) cream

*R*oll out the pastry dough and use it to line a 9-inch (23-cm) pie pan. Flute the edges and set the shell aside in the freezer for 30 minutes or overnight.
❧ Peel the onions, cut them into quarters and slice thin. Heat the butter and oil in a large sauté pan over moderate-low heat. Add the onions and cook, stirring occasionally, until they are golden brown and starting to caramelize, about 30 minutes. Season the onions with salt, pepper and nutmeg.
❧ Preheat an oven to 375°F (190°C). Place the onions in the bottom of the pie shell. In a bowl, beat together the eggs and cream and season with salt and pepper. Pour the mixture over the onions and bake the tart on the middle rack of the oven until set and golden, 30–40 minutes. Let sit for 10 minutes, then slice and serve.

RADICCHIO, FENNEL & WALNUT SALAD

SERVES 6

Italian in style, this pretty salad combines mildly bitter and sweet tastes that nicely counterpoint the onion tart.

3 heads radicchio
3 small fennel bulbs
6 tablespoons (3 fl oz/90 ml) toasted
   walnut oil
2 tablespoons olive oil
3–4 tablespoons balsamic vinegar
salt and freshly ground pepper to taste
1 cup (4 oz/125 g) toasted walnuts
   (see glossary)

*T*rim the ends from the radicchio and separate the leaves. Wash well if sandy and dry well. Remove the tubular stems from the fennel and cut the bulbs into quarters; remove the hard center cores and any discolored outer portions. Slice thin.
❧ In a bowl, combine the walnut oil, olive oil and vinegar to taste with a whisk. Season to taste with salt and pepper. Marinate the walnuts in ¼ cup (2 fl oz/60 ml) of the vinaigrette for 15 minutes. Toss the radicchio, fennel and walnuts in the remaining vinaigrette. Divide among 6 salad plates.

Onion Tart; Radicchio, Fennel & Walnut Salad

RIB-EYE ROAST WITH MUSTARD & BLACK PEPPER

SERVES 6

To ensure perfectly cooked beef, use an instant-read meat thermometer. You should have plenty left over for sandwiches.

FOR THE ROAST:
4–5 lb (2–2.5 kg) rib-eye roast
4 cloves garlic, cut into slivers
1 cup (8 oz/250 g) Dijon mustard
¼ cup (2 fl oz/60 ml) soy sauce
4 tablespoons (2 oz/60 g) coarsely
  ground or cracked pepper

FOR THE SAUCE:
¼ cup (2 oz/60 g) Dijon mustard
1 tablespoon soy sauce
1 cup (8 fl oz/250 ml) beef stock
1 tablespoon cracked pepper

To prepare the roast, cut incisions at even intervals in the surface of the meat and insert slivers of garlic. Place the meat in a roasting pan. Combine the mustard and soy sauce and spread the mixture over the roast. Top with the pepper. Let the roast sit at room temperature for up to 3 hours.

❧ Preheat an oven to 350°F (180°C). Roast the meat until a meat thermometer inserted in the center of the roast reads 120°F (50°C) for rare, about 1½ hours. Remove from the oven and let rest on a carving board, covered with aluminum foil, for 15 minutes.

❧ To make the sauce, in a small pan combine the mustard, soy sauce, beef stock and pepper with a whisk and heat through. Or, pour the stock into the degreased drippings in the roasting pan and stir to free any browned bits. Whisk in the mustard, soy sauce and pepper.

WINTER GREENS WITH PANCETTA & MINT

SERVES 6

Mint and pancetta perfectly offset the mild bitterness of the greens. Make this at the absolute last moment for the freshest color and taste.

¼ cup (2 fl oz/60 ml) olive oil
8 slices bacon or pancetta, about
  ¼ inch (6 mm) thick, cut into dice
  or small strips
1 large onion, chopped, about 2 cups
  (8 oz/250 g)
3 cloves garlic, minced
¼ cup (2 fl oz/60 ml) red wine
  vinegar
1½ lb (750 g) well-washed greens
  (dandelion, kale, chard, mustard
  greens or a combination), stemmed
  and cut into thin strips
salt and freshly ground pepper to taste
6 tablespoons chopped fresh mint

Heat the olive oil in a large sauté pan with high sides. Add the diced bacon or pancetta and cook until translucent but not browned, about 3 minutes. Add the onion and cook until soft, about 8 minutes. Add the garlic and cook for 1–2 minutes. Add the vinegar and greens and cover the pan. Cook the greens until wilted, stirring occasionally, about 5 minutes. Season with salt and pepper and stir in the fresh mint just before serving.

POTATO & SAGE GRATIN

SERVES 6

Fresh sage leaves and a hint of nutmeg perfume this classic dish of sliced and baked potatoes.

3 cups (24 fl oz/750 ml) heavy
  (double) cream
4 cloves garlic, sliced
8–10 fresh sage leaves, chopped, plus
  whole sage leaves for garnish
1½ teaspoons salt
1 teaspoon freshly ground pepper
¼ teaspoon ground nutmeg
6 large white boiling potatoes

Preheat an oven to 375°F (190°C). Butter a 12-cup (3-qt/3-l) baking dish. In a saucepan, bring the cream to a boil with the garlic and sage. Lower the heat and simmer for 15 minutes. Season with salt, pepper and nutmeg.

❧ Peel and slice the potatoes ¼ inch (6 mm) thick. Layer the potatoes in overlapping rows in the baking dish and pour the cream with sage and garlic over them. The cream should just cover the potatoes; if not, add a bit more. Cover with aluminum foil and set aside for up to 2 hours. Bake for 30 minutes, then remove the foil and continue to bake until potatoes are tender but still hold their shape, about 20 minutes longer. Garnish with a few whole sage leaves to serve.

Rib-Eye Roast with Mustard & Black Pepper; Potato & Sage Gratin; Winter Greens with Pancetta & Mint

APPLE CHARLOTTE WITH BRANDIED WHIPPED CREAM & APRICOT SAUCE

SERVES 6

For the most festive presentation, prepare the charlotte in a large mold. The apple purée must be very thick to support the bread casing, so cook it until you get the right consistency.

FOR THE CHARLOTTE:
12 Macintosh, Empire or Rome Beauty
   apples, peeled, cored and cubed
12 tablespoons (6 oz/180 g) unsalted
   butter, melted
¾ cup (6 oz/185 g) granulated sugar
½ teaspoon ground cinnamon
1 tablespoon grated lemon zest
1 teaspoon vanilla extract (essence)
12–15 slices white bread, about ¼
   inch (6 mm) thick, crusts removed

FOR THE BRANDIED WHIPPED CREAM:
1 cup (8 fl oz/250 ml) heavy
   (double) cream
¼ cup (1½ oz/45 g) sifted
   confectioners' (icing) sugar
3 tablespoons brandy, optional

FOR THE APRICOT SAUCE:
1 cup (8 oz/250 g) apricot jam
¼ cup (2 fl oz/60 ml) water
¼ cup (2 fl oz/60 ml) brandy, optional

FOR THE GARNISH:
apricot halves, optional
orange peel, optional

Preheat an oven to 425°F (220°C). In a large, heavy sauté pan over moderate heat, cook the apples with 2 tablespoons of the butter for about 5 minutes. Add the sugar, cinnamon and lemon zest and combine well. Cook until the apples break down into a very thick purée, about 15 minutes. Stir in the vanilla. If the apples are very tart, add a bit more sugar. You should have about 5–6 cups (40–48 fl oz/1.2–1.5 l) apple purée.

❧ Cut the bread into pieces to fit the bottom and sides of a 6-cup (48–fl oz/1.5-l) round charlotte mold or soufflé dish. Dip the bread in the remaining melted butter and place, without overlapping, on the bottom and sides of the mold or dish. Spoon in the apple mixture and top with the remaining bread.

❧ Bake on the lower rack of the oven for 10 minutes, then reduce the oven temperature to 350°F (180°C) and bake until the bread is golden, about 30 minutes longer. Let the charlotte sit for 30 minutes before unmolding. (Or let sit for several hours, then rewarm in a low oven, then unmold.)

❧ To make the brandied whipped cream, in a bowl beat the cream and sugar until it forms soft peaks. Fold in the brandy, if desired. To make the apricot sauce, stir together the jam and water in a small saucepan and warm over low heat. Stir in the brandy if desired. Top the charlotte with some of the whipped cream and serve with the remaining whipped cream and the apricot sauce. Garnish with the apricot halves and orange peel, if desired.

Gold tones set the theme for a beguiling display of presents. Yet these elegant touches need not be costly. Use widely available Christmas ribbon, beads and ornaments in amber hues. To make pine cones gleam like treasures, spray them lightly with gold paint. Tuck a favorite card in a gilded mirror or picture frame.

Apple Charlotte with Brandied Whipped Cream & Apricot Sauce

New Year's Eve for Six

With the new year comes a spirit of optimism and an eager anticipation of new achievements, of resolutions soon to be fulfilled. As a result, New Year's Eve celebrations can be the most sparkling events of the year. This is a good time to invite your closest friends for a celebratory evening that doesn't end until well after midnight.

To observe New Year's Eve in style, we planned a sit-down dinner for six, to be served late in the evening. We selected elegant floral arrangements, including white tulips, roses, narcissus and orchids with green hydrangeas and bay laurel, but you can use any kind of blossoms, greens or potted plants to make the setting as informal or formal as you wish. A party favor, wrapped in silver foil and streamers, adds intrigue to each place setting.

Menu

Duck Livers with Apple-Ginger Butter

Rice Croquettes

———

Winter Bouillabaisse

Green Salad

———

Blood Orange Crème Brûlée

Ginger Florentines

To highlight the once-a-year mood of New Year's, we chose to splurge with a menu featuring duck livers, lobster, shrimp, scallops and crème brûlée, the richest of custards. The star of the meal is a hands-on bouillabaisse, the classic Provençal fish soup. For this course, you might want to provide your guests with oversized bib napkins to use.

To help you put together this special meal, consult the preparation list at right and the tips given with each recipe. The soup can be prepared in steps so that the last-minute cooking is minimal. You could also serve fewer dishes or add recipes from other menus in this book. The most important thing is to plan the evening so that you can enjoy the revelries as much as your guests.

WINE RECOMMENDATIONS

Start with a non-vintage brut Champagne, a California sparkling wine, or Cava from Spain. Follow with either a Chardonnay-based cuvée Champagne, or, if you want a still wine, a bracing white such as French Muscadet or Chablis. With dessert and midnight toasting, pour an extra-dry or demi-sec sparkling wine or Champagne.

A richly polished dining table reflects the elegance of fine silver, china, crystal and white floral arrangements. Left, a side table holds a silver coffee service.

PREPARATION LIST

• The day before, prepare the apple-ginger butter; assemble the croquettes; make the florentines and store them in an airtight container.

• The morning of the party, make the soup base, prepare and refrigerate the aïoli and the rouille and clean the seafood for the bouillabaisse. Make the crème brûlée custard.

• One hour before, prepare the potatoes, fennel and bread for the soup.

• Fifteen minutes before guests arrive, cook the livers and croquettes. Bring the soup base to a simmer. Just before serving, finish the soup and the crème brûlée.

EACH RECIPE YIELDS 6 SERVINGS

A silver mint julep cup serves as a vase for narcissus. The leather-bound books and small wooden chest create a casually elegant shelf.

DUCK LIVERS WITH APPLE-GINGER BUTTER

SERVES 6

Perfumed by the apples and ginger, the duck livers make an unforgettable hors d'oeuvre for a special occasion.

about 6 tablespoons (3 oz/90 g) unsalted butter
1 small apple, peeled, cored and finely chopped
one 2-inch (5-cm) piece fresh ginger, peeled and grated
2 tablespoons Calvados (apple-flavored brandy)
salt and freshly ground pepper to taste
12 large duck or chicken livers

In a small sauté pan, melt 2 tablespoons of the butter. Add the apple and ginger and cook until the apple is very soft, about 10–15 minutes. Add the Calvados and cook 1–2 minutes longer. Transfer the mixture to a blender or food processor and purée. Add about 4 tablespoons (2 oz/60 g) of the remaining butter or enough to make a thick, creamy compound. Season with salt and pepper. This butter may be made up to 1 day ahead of time, covered and refrigerated, then softened at room temperature before serving.

❧ Trim the livers carefully of fat and sinew; thread on skewers and sprinkle with salt and pepper. Preheat a broiler (griller). Broil the livers, turning once, until browned on the outside and medium rare in the center, about 2 minutes on each side. Remove the livers from the skewers, place 2 on each plate and top equally with the apple-ginger butter.

RICE CROQUETTES

MAKES 12–16 CROQUETTES

In Italy, these croquettes are known as supplì al telefono, or "telephone wires," which aptly describes the strings formed by biting into their cheese filling.

2 cups (16 fl oz/500 ml) lightly salted water
1 cup (7 oz/220 g) Arborio rice
2 eggs, beaten
5 tablespoons (1¼ oz/35 g) freshly grated Parmesan cheese
salt, freshly ground pepper and ground nutmeg to taste
8 ounces (250 g) fresh mozzarella cheese, cut into 12–16 small cubes
1 tablespoon chopped fresh marjoram or sage
¾ cup (3 oz/90 g) dried bread crumbs
peanut oil for deep-frying

In a saucepan, bring the water to a boil and stir in the rice; reduce heat and simmer, covered, until it has absorbed all the water and is cooked through but still sticky, about 20 minutes. Stir in the eggs and Parmesan and season with salt, pepper and nutmeg. Spread out evenly in an oiled baking sheet with sides and cool in the refrigerator.

❧ Line a baking sheet with baking parchment and set aside. Roll the cheese cubes in the chopped herb. Scoop up a heaping tablespoonful of the rice, make a well in it and tuck a piece of mozzarella in the center. Push the rice over the cheese and form it into a ball about 1½ inches (4 cm) in diameter. Repeat until all the rice is used. Dip the croquettes in the bread crumbs, place on the lined baking sheet and refrigerate until just before serving (up to 1 day).

❧ To serve, heat about 3 inches (7.5 cm) of peanut oil in a deep-fat fryer or wok to 350°F (180°C). Drop in a few croquettes at a time and fry until golden brown, lifting them in and out of the oil a few times with a slotted spoon so that the cheese will have time to melt in the center before the croquettes get too brown. Drain on paper towels and keep warm in a low oven for no more than 10 minutes before serving. Repeat until all the croquettes are cooked; serve at once.

New Year's Eve is synonymous with effervescence, so position iced champagne and several crystal flutes near the entryway, then pour a welcoming glassful for each guest as he or she arrives.

Rice Croquettes; Duck Livers with Apple-Ginger Butter

Winter Bouillabaisse

SERVES 6

While shellfish are not traditionally used in bouillabaisse, for New Year's Eve they make it seem especially festive. Depending on your budget, use as much as you can afford. If you don't eat shellfish, leave it out and increase the fish to 3 pounds (1.5 kg) total.

The key to success with this dish is organization. Make the soup base, rouille and aïoli the morning of the party and boil the lobster and crab (or purchase already cooked ones from your fishmonger), then prepare all the fish and shellfish and chill it (debeard mussels just before cooking). Get all the ingredients for the accompaniments ready, too; these can be cooked up to an hour before eating. At the last minute, reheat the soup base, add the seafood and your main course is ready.

FOR THE SOUP BASE:

¼ cup (2 fl oz/60 ml) olive oil
2 leeks, cut in half lengthwise and rinsed well, thinly sliced
2 large onions, diced, about 2 cups (8 oz/250 g)
2–3 ribs celery, diced
6 cloves garlic, minced
3–4 strips orange zest, ½ inch (12 mm) wide and 3 inches (7.5 cm) long
¼ teaspoon saffron threads, steeped in ¼ cup (2 fl oz/60 ml) white wine
12 fresh thyme sprigs
2 bay leaves
1 tablespoon ground fennel seed
½–1 teaspoon red pepper flakes
3 cups (1⅛ lb/560 g) drained and diced canned plum tomatoes
12 cups (3 qt/3 l) fish stock (see recipe on page 175) or 6 cups (48 fl oz/1.5 l) *each* chicken stock and bottled clam juice
salt and freshly ground pepper to taste

FOR THE ROUILLE:

3 slices bread, crusts removed, torn up
4 cloves garlic, minced very fine
1 teaspoon cayenne pepper
2 tablespoons tomato paste
6 tablespoons (3 fl oz/90 ml) olive oil
fish stock or bottled clam juice as needed

FOR THE BOUILLABAISSE:

2 lb (1 kg) boneless, skinless angler, flounder, bass or snapper cut into 3- by 2-inch (7.5- by 5-cm) chunks
1 live Atlantic (Maine) lobster, 1½ lb (750 g), boiled for 10 minutes, cleaned, cracked and cut into chunks
1 large crab, boiled for 10 minutes, cleaned, cracked and cut into chunks
18 large shrimp, shelled and deveined
18 sea scallops
about 1 cup dry white wine
2 lb (1 kg) mussels, scrubbed well and debearded
½ cup (¾ oz/20 g) chopped fresh parsley
¼ cup (⅜ oz/10 g) chopped fennel fronds

FOR THE ACCOMPANIMENTS:

3 fennel bulbs, quartered, cored and blanched until tender
18 very small potatoes, boiled
12 slices toasted French bread, rubbed with garlic
1 cup (8 oz/250 g) aïoli (recipe on page 174), optional

To make the soup base, heat the olive oil in a large, heavy pot. Add the leeks, onions and celery and cook until tender, about 10–15 minutes. Add the garlic, orange zest, saffron and wine, thyme, bay leaves, fennel seed, red pepper flakes, tomatoes and stock and bring to a boil. Reduce the heat and simmer until flavors are melded, about 15 minutes. Season with salt and pepper. You may refrigerate this, uncovered, until serving time.

To make the rouille, combine the bread, garlic, cayenne and tomato paste in a blender or food processor. With the motor running, gradually pour in the oil. Transfer to a bowl and stir in enough fish stock or clam juice to make a spoonable sauce. Cover and refrigerate until serving time.

To make the bouillabaisse, bring the soup base to a simmer. Add the fish and cook about 2 minutes; add the lobster, crab and shrimp and cook 2 minutes longer, then add the scallops and cook until all the seafood is firm, about 2 minutes longer. Meanwhile, in a large sauté pan, bring the wine to a boil. Add the mussels, reduce the heat, cover and steam until the mussels open, about 6–8 minutes; discard any unopened mussels. Add the mussels and their cooking liquid to the bouillabaisse. Ladle into soup bowls and top with chopped parsley and fennel fronds. Serve the rouille, fennel, potatoes, French bread and, if using, aïoli, in bowls alongside to add as desired.

After the soup, you could offer a fresh salad of mixed winter greens including crisp lettuces, frisée and radicchio.

Winter Bouillabaisse

Blood Orange Crème Brulée; Ginger Florentines

BLOOD ORANGE CRÈME BRULEE

SERVES 6

Use regular oranges if you can't find blood oranges for this extra-rich custard.

1 cup (8 fl oz/250 ml) fresh-squeezed
   blood orange or regular orange juice
½ cup (4 fl oz/125 ml) Grand Marnier
   or other orange-flavored liqueur
2 cups (16 fl oz/500 ml) heavy
   (double) cream
grated zest of 2 blood oranges or
   regular oranges
¾ cup (6 oz/185 g) plus 2 tablespoons sugar
6 egg yolks, beaten

*I*n a small saucepan, combine the orange juice and liqueur and cook over high heat to reduce to ½ cup (4 fl oz/ 125 ml). Set aside. In another small saucepan, combine the cream, orange zest and 6 tablespoons of the sugar. Bring to a simmer, stirring, over moderate heat. Remove from heat and cover. Let steep for 30 minutes.

ॐ Preheat an oven to 300°F (150°C). Place the egg yolks in a bowl and stir in the cream mixture. Add the juice and liqueur. Pour the mixture into one 5-cup (40–fl oz/1.2-l) shallow baking dish or six small (6–fl oz/180 ml) ramekins. Place in a baking pan and add hot water to come halfway up the sides of the custard container(s). Bake until just set, 45–60 minutes. Remove from the baking pan and place in the refrigerator. When cold, cover and chill thoroughly.

ॐ To serve, preheat a broiler (griller). Sprinkle the remaining sugar over the custard(s). Place under a very hot broiler until the sugar has caramelized, about 3–4 minutes. Let sit until the melted sugar has hardened, then serve.

GINGER FLORENTINES

MAKES 12 DOUBLE COOKIES

Candied ginger adds an exotic flair to these crisp-textured, lacy cookies.

4 tablespoons (2 oz/60 g) unsalted butter
1½ cups (6 oz/185 g) sliced almonds
½ cup (4 oz/125 g) sugar
⅓ cup (3 fl oz/90 ml) heavy (double) cream
¼ cup (3 oz/90 g) honey
¼ cup (1 oz/30 g) chopped candied
   orange peel
¼ cup (1½ oz/45 g) candied ginger
½ teaspoon vanilla extract (essence)
¼ teaspoon ground cinnamon
¼ cup (1½ oz/45 g) all-purpose
   (plain) flour
4 oz (125 g) bittersweet chocolate

*P*reheat an oven to 325°F (170°C). In a small saucepan, melt 2 tablespoons of the butter. Line 2 baking sheets with baking parchment and brush the paper with the melted butter. Chop 1 cup (4 oz/125 g) of the almonds. Finely chop the remaining almonds in a food processor or blender; do not let it turn to paste.

ॐ In a small, deep saucepan, place the sugar, cream, honey and remaining 2 tablespoons butter. Bring to a boil, stirring once or twice, and cook until a candy thermometer reads 238°F (114°C). Stir in the candied orange peel, candied ginger, vanilla, cinnamon, flour and almonds. Let cool; then drop by the teaspoonful onto the baking sheets, leaving 3 inches (7.5 cm) between each cookie. Flatten with a fork or spread out with a spoon.

ॐ Bake until golden brown, about 12 minutes. Let cool on the pans for several minutes, then transfer to racks. Meanwhile, melt the chocolate in the top of a double boiler over simmering water. Coat one side of each cookie with chocolate and top with a second cookie.

New Year's Buffet

The first day of the new year calls for entertaining of the most relaxed kind. With that in mind, we planned a late-lunch party of familiar, easy-to-eat foods that could be enjoyed while watching televised parades or sports. Whether served midday or in early evening, it's easiest to set the dishes on a coffee table near the fire or the television and let guests serve themselves. To promote a cozier feeling, we pulled in sofas and chairs from around the room.

In keeping with the casual feel of this menu, everyday dishware, cutlery and napkins are the best choice; stack them close by the food. There's no need to fuss over decorations, either. We used a few palm fronds and banana leaves to bring a touch of tropical warmth to the room and incorporated them into the personal artifacts already on display.

Menu

Quesadillas

Black Bean Soup
with Dark Rum & Orange Zest

———

Barbecued Chicken Sandwiches

Sweet & White Potato Gratin

Spinach Salad
with Pecans & Balsamic Vinaigrette

———

Chocolate Pound Cake

This buffet menu is particularly appealing for holiday entertaining because most of it can be made ahead and finished just before the guests arrive. These dishes are so versatile, you also could serve them for a New Year's Eve party, an après-ski gathering or a Sunday supper. In fact, any chilly day of the year would be appropriate for this medley of soup, salad and sandwiches.

You could begin the meal with bowls of black bean soup set atop dinner plates; place the quesadillas alongside. These plates can then be used for the sandwiches, potatoes and salad, while dessert can be eaten out of hand. The plan for this party is to make life easy for both the guests and the host, a great way to start the year.

WINE RECOMMENDATIONS

To complement the somewhat spicy food, select a slightly smoky red wine loaded with ripe fruit, such as Zinfandel or Burgundy. If you wish to continue toasting the new year, pour a rose Champagne or sparkling wine. Beer is also a good choice for this meal; choose a medium-bodied amber ale or lager. For dessert, add a dash of Kahlúa to the coffee.

A wooden planter set on the deck or moved inside becomes an ice chest for beer and mineral water. Left, set out some classic games, along with mugs of coffee and dessert, to amuse guests all afternoon long.

PREPARATION LIST

• Up to 1 month ahead, make the barbecue sauce and refrigerate in a tightly covered container.

• The day before, make the soup and bake the pound cake.

• The morning of the party, wash and stem the spinach and prepare the dressing; assemble the quesadillas, to be fried before serving.

• Up to several hours before, assemble and bake the potato gratin, to be rewarmed before serving.

EACH RECIPE YIELDS 12 SERVINGS

A serene study in Asian artifacts is an oasis of calm.

QUESADILLAS

SERVES 12

One of the great snacks of Mexico, these filled tortillas are the Latin American equivalent of the grilled cheese sandwich.

6 large fresh poblano chili peppers
6 ripe avocados
6 cups (1½ lb/750 g) grated Monterey
 jack cheese
24 flour tortillas
2 cups (6 oz/185 g) finely chopped
 green (spring) onions
½ cup (¾ oz/20 g) finely chopped
 cilantro (fresh coriander)
salt and freshly ground pepper to taste
salsa, optional

*R*oast, peel and derib the peppers as directed on page 189. Cut the flesh into ¼-inch (6-mm) dice.
❧ Cut the avocados in half, remove the pit, scoop from the shell with a large spoon and cut into thin slices.
❧ Spread about ¼ cup (1 oz/30 g) grated cheese over half of each tortilla. Top equally with some diced peppers, a few slices of avocado, the minced green onions and cilantro; sprinkle with salt and pepper. Fold each tortilla gently in half without pressing down on it or it will crack. Repeat until all the ingredients are used. Cover and refrigerate until ready to cook (up to several hours)
❧ Place a griddle or large frying pan over medium-high heat and lightly oil it. Place as many filled tortillas as can fit on the griddle or in the pan, weight slightly with a pan lid and cook until golden brown on each side, turning once. Repeat until all the quesadillas are cooked. If desired, cut each quesadilla in half and serve with salsa.

BLACK BEAN SOUP WITH DARK RUM & ORANGE ZEST

SERVES 12

Robust and warming, this Caribbean-style soup gains an unusual twist from rum and citrus.

6 cups (2½ lb/1.25 kg) dried
 black beans
12 cups (3 qt/3 l) cold water
1 ham bone or hock or prosciutto bone
3 tablespoons olive oil
3 large onions, diced, about 6 cups
 (1½ lb/750 g)
8 cloves garlic, minced
1½ teaspoons ground cinnamon
½ teaspoon ground cloves
1 teaspoon ground cumin
2 teaspoons dry mustard dissolved in
 1 tablespoon sherry vinegar
2 tablespoons grated orange zest
½ cup (4 fl oz/125 ml) dark rum
1 cup (8 fl oz/250 ml) fresh
 orange juice
salt and freshly ground pepper to taste
sour cream, optional
thin slices of orange, optional

*P*ick over the beans to remove any debris. Soak the beans overnight in water to cover amply. Drain. Place the beans in a large pot, add the cold water and the hock or bone and bring to a boil. Reduce the heat to a simmer.
❧ In a large sauté pan, heat the olive oil. Add the onions and cook until tender, about 10 minutes. Add the garlic, cinnamon, cloves, cumin, mustard mixed with vinegar, and orange zest and cook 2 more minutes. Add this mixture to the beans. Cook, partially covered, until the beans are very ten-

der, about 60 minutes. Remove the bone or ham hock and discard. Purée the soup in batches in a blender or a food processor. If desired, cool, cover and refrigerate for up to 1 day.
❧ Return the soup to the heat and bring to a boil. Stir in the rum and orange juice. Season well with salt and pepper. Ladle into bowls and garnish each serving with sour cream and a thin slice of orange, if desired.

*P*lan on potting flowering bulbs in
a large urn or stoneware vase early
in the season so they'll be in full
bloom on New Year's Day.

Quesadillas; Black Bean Soup with Dark Rum & Orange Zest

BARBECUED CHICKEN SANDWICHES

MAKES 12 SANDWICHES

Serve the sandwiches either open-faced or closed, slathered with as much barbecue sauce as you like. If made without the optional orange or lemon juice, this sauce will keep for several months under refrigeration.

FOR THE BARBECUE SAUCE:

2 tablespoons dry mustard

3 tablespoons chili powder

1 teaspoon ground ginger

½ cup (4 fl oz/125 ml) cider vinegar

1½ cups (12 fl oz/375 ml) tomato purée (see glossary)

2 tablespoons Worcestershire sauce

½ cup (3½ oz/105 g) light brown sugar, packed

½ cup (4 fl oz/125 ml) fresh orange juice or ¼ cup (2 fl oz/60 ml) fresh lemon juice, optional

1 tablespoon freshly ground pepper

cayenne pepper and salt to taste

FOR THE SANDWICHES:

12 boneless, skinless chicken breast halves

12 sandwich rolls, such as Kaiser rolls or poppy-seed rolls

To make the barbecue sauce, in a small bowl combine the mustard, chili powder and ginger and moisten with some of the vinegar. When smooth and dissolved, add the remaining vinegar. In a medium saucepan, stir together the tomato purée, Worcestershire sauce, brown sugar and, if desired, orange or lemon juice. Whisk in the vinegar mixture. Bring to a boil, reduce heat and simmer for 5 minutes. If the sauce seems too thick, thin it with a little water. Season with the ground pepper,

cayenne and salt to taste. Cover and refrigerate until ready to serve.

🥄 To make the sandwiches, preheat a broiler (griller) and broil the chicken breasts, brushing occasionally with the barbecue sauce, until cooked through, about 3 minutes on each side. Reheat the barbecue sauce in a small saucepan. Cut the chicken into ¼-inch (6-mm) slices. Dip in the sauce and place on the rolls. Or, serve the sauce alongside.

SWEET & WHITE POTATO GRATIN

SERVES 12

Its slight edge of sweetness makes this side dish of sliced and baked potatoes a nice complement to the barbecue sandwiches.

6 cups (48 fl oz/1.5 l) heavy (double) cream

6 cloves garlic, smashed with the flat of a knife

salt, freshly ground pepper and ground nutmeg to taste

6 large russet potatoes

6 large yams

Preheat an oven to 375°F (190°C). In a saucepan, bring the cream to a boil with the garlic, lower the heat and simmer for 10 minutes. Remove the garlic and season the cream with salt, pepper and nutmeg to taste. The mixture should be a little salty, as the potatoes are very bland and will absorb the cream and salt.

🥄 While the cream is simmering, peel and slice the potatoes and yams ¼ inch (6 mm) thick. Layer the potatoes and yams in overlapping rows in a deep baking dish or lasagne pan. Pour the warm cream over the potatoes and

yams. The cream should just cover the potatoes; if not, add a bit more. Bake until the potatoes and yams are tender, about 45 minutes.

SPINACH SALAD WITH PECANS & BALSAMIC VINAIGRETTE

SERVES 12

By mixing two types of olive oil for the dressing, you get a more balanced flavor for this light spinach salad.

6–8 bunches small-leafed spinach

1 bunch green (spring) onions, sliced thin

½ cup (4 fl oz/125 ml) olive oil

¼ cup (2 fl oz/60 ml) extra-virgin olive oil

⅓ cup (3 fl oz/90 ml) balsamic vinegar

salt and freshly ground pepper to taste

2 cups (8 oz/250 g) toasted pecans (see glossary)

3 ripe pears, cored and sliced, optional (peels may be left on)

Remove the stems from the spinach, rinse the leaves well and pat dry. You should have about 18 cups loosely packed leaves (about 12 oz/375 g). If desired, refrigerate the spinach in a plastic bag for several hours.

🥄 To serve, combine the spinach and green onions in a large salad bowl. In another bowl, whisk together the olive oils and vinegar and season with salt and pepper. Toss the pecans in ½ cup (4 fl oz/125 ml) of the vinaigrette. Add the pecans and the optional pears to the spinach. Dress the salad with the remaining vinaigrette, toss well and serve at once.

Barbecued Chicken Sandwiches; Sweet & White Potato Gratin; Spinach Salad with Pecans & Balsamic Vinaigrette

CHOCOLATE POUND CAKE

MAKES ONE 9- BY 5- BY 3-INCH
(23- BY 13- BY 7.5-CM) CAKE

*Dust the pound cake with powdered sugar
if you wish. To serve, slice it to be eaten
by hand, or serve on plates topped with
whipped cream or ice cream.*

1½ cups (6 oz/185 g) sifted all-purpose
  (plain) flour
½ cup (2 oz/60 g) sifted unsweetened
  Dutch-process cocoa
¼ teaspoon salt
2 oz (60 g) bittersweet chocolate
1 cup (8 oz/250 g) unsalted butter at
  room temperature
2 cups (14 oz/440g) light brown
  sugar, packed
3 eggs
1 teaspoon vanilla extract (essence)
1 cup (8 oz/250 g) sour cream

Preheat an oven to 350°F (180°C).
Butter a 9- by 5- by 3-inch (23- by
13- by 7.5-cm) loaf pan. Sift the flour,
cocoa and salt together. Set aside. Place
the chocolate in the top of a double
boiler and melt over simmering water.
⁓ In a large bowl, beat the butter and
brown sugar together until fluffy. Beat
in the eggs, one at a time. Add the
vanilla and the melted chocolate and
mix well. Fold a third of the dry ingredients, then half the sour cream into the
chocolate mixture; repeat, ending with
the dry ingredients. Pour the batter into
the prepared loaf pan.
⁓ Bake until a toothpick inserted in
the center of the cake comes out clean,
about 1 hour. If the cake is browning
too quickly, cover it loosely with
aluminum foil. Let the cake cool in the
pan on a rack for 10 minutes, then turn
out onto the rack to cool completely.
Slice and serve.

*Arrange personal collectibles with
tropical or regular greenery on a side
table for an eye-catching decoration.*

Chocolate Pound Cake

BASIC RECIPES

Throughout this book, you'll find recipes that call for stocks to moisten and flavor soups and stews; breads to accompany meals and lend body and texture to other dishes; and pastry that serves as the foundation for a variety of sweet and savory pies.

When entertaining at home, you may want to make these staples from scratch to add distinction to your special menus. If your schedule is tight, do not hesitate to substitute a store-bought item instead. Good canned and frozen stocks, as well as refrigerated pie pastry, are available in quality food stores. The rise of boutique bakeries makes it even easier to find excellent bread and you can replicate the flavor of aïoli by mixing pressed garlic with commercial mayonnaise.

AÏOLI

A traditional garlic-laced mayonnaise from the region of Provence in France, where it is served with cooked vegetables and potatoes as a dip. This recipe contains raw eggs; for more information, see page 187.

1 tablespoon finely chopped garlic
½ teaspoon salt
2 large egg yolks
3–4 tablespoons fresh lemon juice
2 cups (16 fl oz/500 ml) olive oil

Place the garlic and the salt in a mortar and grind it to a fine paste with the pestle. Put the egg yolks in a blender or food processor. Add 3 tablespoons of the lemon juice and blend. With the machine running, gradually add the olive oil a few drops at a time until the sauce is emulsified, then slowly add the remaining oil. Add the prepared garlic paste. Add more lemon juice and salt if desired. Transfer to a bowl, cover and refrigerate for up to 8 hours.

Makes about 2½ cups (20 fl oz/625 ml)

BEEF STOCK

Incomparably rich and deep in color, this stock will add an intense depth of flavor to soups, stews and sauces. It takes all day to simmer, but you don't have to hover over the stove while it's cooking.

6 lb (3 kg) meaty beef shanks (shins)
10 cups (2½ qt/2.5 l) cold water
beef scraps or other trimmings, optional
2 yellow onions, coarsely chopped
1 leek, trimmed, carefully washed and coarsely chopped
2 carrots, peeled and coarsely chopped
1 celery stalk, coarsely chopped
about 1 cup (8 fl oz/250 ml) hot water
6 cloves garlic
4 fresh parsley sprigs
10 whole peppercorns
3 fresh thyme sprigs
2 small bay leaves

Preheat an oven to 450°F (230°C). Place the beef shanks in a roasting pan and roast, turning occasionally, until browned, about 1½ hours. Transfer the shanks with tongs to a large stockpot and add the cold water. Add beef scraps, if using. Bring to a boil and skim off any scum on the surface. Reduce the heat to a simmer and cook, uncovered, adding water as needed to keep the bones submerged. Skim the surface occasionally.

Meanwhile, place the roasting pan on the stovetop. Add the onions, leek, carrots and celery to the pan. Cook over high heat, stirring often, until the vegetables are browned, about 20 minutes. Add the vegetables to the stockpot. Pour the hot water into the roasting pan, bring to a simmer and stir to dislodge any browned bits. Add to the stockpot.

Place the garlic, parsley sprigs, peppercorns, thyme sprigs and bay leaves on a square of cheese-cloth (muslin) and tie up with cotton string. Add to the stockpot. Simmer the stock, uncovered, over low heat, at least 6–8 hours, or preferably all day.

Remove the stockpot from the heat and lift out the solids with a slotted spoon. Strain the liquid into a bowl through a strainer lined with cheesecloth (muslin). Discard the solids. Let the stock cool to room temperature, then cover and refrigerate until cold. Lift or spoon off the solidified fat on top and discard. Store the stock in one or more tightly covered containers in the refrigerator for up to several days or in the freezer for up to 6 months.

Makes about 2½ qt (2.5 l)

CHICKEN STOCK

The all-purpose kitchen standby, homemade chicken stock is the best for soups, stews, risottos and so many other recipes. Adding salt to taste to the finished broth lets you control the flavor desired.

1 leek, trimmed and carefully washed

6 lb (3 kg) stewing chicken parts

1 large yellow onion, unpeeled, root trimmed

1 large carrot, peeled and cut into 1-inch (2.5-cm) chunks

1 celery stalk with leaves, cut into 1-inch (2.5-cm) chunks

6 fresh parsley sprigs

3 fresh thyme sprigs

1 bay leaf

½ teaspoon peppercorns

5 qt (5 l) water

salt to taste

Cut the leek into 1-inch (2.5-cm) chunks and place in a large stockpot. Add the chicken, onion, carrot and celery to the pot. Place the parsley, thyme, bay leaf and peppercorns on a square of cheesecloth (muslin) and tie up with cotton string. Add to the pot with the water.

Over low to moderate heat, slowly bring the liquid to a simmer, skimming off the scum that rises to the surface. Cover partially and continue simmering gently for about 2 hours, skimming occasionally.

Strain into a large bowl through a strainer lined with cheesecloth (muslin). Discard the solids. Season with salt and let cool to room temperature, then cover and refrigerate until cold. Lift or spoon off the solidified fat on top and discard. Store the stock in one or more tightly covered containers in the refrigerator for up to several days or in the freezer for up to 6 months.
Makes about 4 qt (4 l)

FISH STOCK

Delicate and quick-cooking, fish stock, or fumet, is the basis for successful fish soups and stews. Ask your fishmonger for fish frames, or buy a whole fish and have the fillets removed for you to use in another recipe.

6–8 lb (3–4 kg) fish frames (bones) with heads and tails (gills removed) from mild flavored fish such as snapper, rockfish or halibut

2 tablespoons olive oil

8 cups (64 fl oz/2 l) water or to cover

3 cups (24 fl oz/750 ml) dry white wine

3 yellow onions, chopped

4 celery stalks, chopped

3 strips lemon zest

5 fresh parsley sprigs

2 fresh thyme sprigs

10 peppercorns

4 coriander seeds

3 allspice berries

1 bay leaf

Rinse the fish frames well. Heat the olive oil in a large, heavy pot over moderate heat and cook the fish frames, stirring often, until they give off some liquid, about 10 minutes.

Add the water, wine, onions and celery. Place the lemon zest, parsley sprigs, thyme sprigs, peppercorns, coriander seeds, allspice and bay leaf on a square of cheesecloth (muslin) and tie up with string. Add to the stockpot and bring to a boil. Reduce the heat and simmer, uncovered, for 30 minutes, skimming the scum from the surface occasionally. Strain into a bowl through a strainer lined with cheesecloth (muslin). Discard the solids. Let the stock cool to room temperature, then cover and refrigerate until cold. Store in a tightly covered container in the refrigerator for 1–2 days, or transfer to one or more tightly covered containers and store in the freezer for up to 6 months.
Makes about 2½ qt (2.5 l)

BAGUETTES

Slender batons of homemade bread are the quintessential accompaniment to many European meals. This is one of the easiest breads of all to make. To ensure a crisp crust, spray the bread lightly with a water mister 3 or 4 times during the first 10 minutes of baking.

1 tablespoon active dry yeast

2½ cups (20 fl oz/625 ml) warm
(110°F/43°C) water

6 cups (30 oz/940 g) unbleached
all-purpose (plain) flour

1 tablespoon salt

Dissolve the yeast in the warm water in the bowl of an electric mixer (or in a large bowl). Gradually add the flour and salt and mix with the paddle attachment to combine (or beat with a wooden spoon). Change to the dough hook and knead on moderate speed (or knead by hand on a lightly floured board) until the dough is smooth and elastic, 5 to 10 minutes, adding more flour as necessary to prevent sticking. Transfer the dough to an oiled bowl, cover with a towel and let rise in a warm place until doubled in size, about 1 hour. Punch down the dough, cover and refrigerate overnight.

The next day, remove the dough from the refrigerator and allow it to rest for 1 hour. Shape into 3 baguettes; place the baguettes on baking sheets. Cover with kitchen towels and let rise in a warm place until doubled in size, about 1 hour.

Preheat an oven to 425°F (220°C). With a sharp knife or razor blade, cut several diagonal slashes in the top of each baguette. Bake until golden brown, about 20 minutes, spraying the bread with a water mister 3 or 4 times during the first 10 minutes of baking. Remove from the oven and let the baguettes cool on racks.

Makes three 1-lb (500-g) loaves

COUNTRY BREAD

Known as pane integrale *in Italian, this bread gets a distinctive tang from a sourdough-like starter. You can double the starter and make enough for future loaves of bread.*

For the Starter:

1 cup (8 fl oz/250 ml) warm (110°F/43°C)
water

⅛ teaspoon active dry yeast

2 cups (10 oz/315 g) unbleached
all-purpose (plain) flour

For the Bread:

1 tablespoon active dry yeast

2¼ cups (18 fl oz/560 ml) warm
(110°F/43°C) water

2 tablespoons olive oil

¾ cup (3 oz/90 g) pumpernickel rye meal
or dark rye flour

¾ cup (4 oz/125 g) coarse whole-wheat
(wholemeal) flour

4¾ cups (1½ lb/750 g) unbleached
all-purpose (plain) flour

1 tablespoon salt

To make the starter, place the warm water, yeast and flour in the bowl of an electric mixer (or a large bowl) and beat with the paddle attachment at medium speed for 3 minutes or until the starter pulls away from sides of the bowl (or beat with a wooden spoon). Place the starter in a 4-qt (4-l) plastic container or any container large enough to allow the starter to triple in size. Cover and let sit at room temperature overnight. Use the next day or, preferably, refrigerate for 1–2 days longer to develop the flavor.

To make the bread, place the yeast and the starter with the warm water in the bowl of an electric mixer (or in a large bowl). Mix with the paddle attachment until it is dissolved, about 5 minutes (or beat with a wooden spoon). The mixture will be chalky white and foamy.

Change to the dough hook and add (or stir in) the olive oil, rye meal, whole-wheat flour, all-purpose flour and salt. Knead on moderate speed until you have a stiff, firm dough that pulls completely away from the side of the bowl; continue kneading for 5 minutes (or knead by hand on a lightly floured board) until smooth and elastic, adding more all-purpose flour as necessary to prevent sticking. Transfer the dough to an oiled bowl, cover and refrigerate overnight.

The next day, shape the dough into 2 loaves and place on greased baking sheets, or place in greased loaf pans. Cover with kitchen towels and let rise in a warm place until doubled in size, about 1½–2 hours.

Preheat an oven to 450°F (230°C). With a sharp knife or razor blade, cut 3 diagonal slashes in the top of each loaf. Place in the oven, reduce the heat to 400°F (200°C) and bake until golden brown, 45–60 minutes, spraying the bread with a water mister about 4 times during the first 20 minutes. Remove bread from the oven and let cool on racks.

Makes two 1¾-lb (875-g) loaves

BASIC PIE PASTRY

Use this recipe for a fail-safe crust for the pies in this book. If you want a sweet crust, add the sugar; for savory pies, leave it out. To achieve a flaky texture, make it with butter; for tender crusts, use the vegetable shortening, or use half of each. After rolling out the dough and placing it in the pan, put it in the freezer to rest for at least 30 minutes so that it will shrink less in baking.

For a Single-Crust Pie Shell:

½ cup (4 oz/125 g) chilled unsalted butter or vegetable shortening (vegetable lard), or half of each

1½ cups (7½ oz/235 g) all-purpose (plain) flour

½ teaspoon salt

1 tablespoon sugar, optional

about 3–4 tablespoons cold water

For a Double-Crust Pie Shell or 2 Pie Crusts:

¾ cup (6 oz/180 g) chilled unsalted butter or vegetable shortening (vegetable lard), or half of each

2¼ cups (11½ oz/360 g) all-purpose (plain) flour

¾ teaspoon salt

2 tablespoons sugar, optional

about 6–7 tablespoons (3–3½ fl oz/90–95 ml) cold water

HAND METHOD

Cut the butter or shortening into small pieces. Combine the flour, salt and, if using, sugar in a medium bowl. Add the butter or shortening. With your fingertips, 2 knives or a pastry blender, quickly blend the ingredients together until the mixture resembles coarse crumbs. Sprinkle on the water 1 tablespoon at a time. Stir with a fork after each addition, adding just enough water for the dough to mass together. Turn out onto a lightly floured board and, with floured hands, pat the dough into 1 or 2 smooth disks. Make one just slightly larger than the other if you are preparing a double-crust pie. Roll out the dough and place it in the pan as directed in the recipe of your choice. Put the pie shell in the freezer and let it rest for at least 30 minutes before baking.

FOOD PROCESSOR METHOD

Cut the butter or shortening into large pieces. With the steel blade attached, place the flour, salt, sugar (if using) and butter or shortening in the work bowl. Process with rapid off-on pulses until the mixture resembles cornmeal; do not overprocess or the pastry will be tough. Add the water, a little at a time, and process until blended; do not let the mixture form a ball. Stop and feel the dough (taking care not to touch the blade); it should be just damp enough to mass together. If necessary, add more water by teaspoonfuls, processing for just an instant after each addition. Turn out onto a lightly floured board and, with floured hands, pat the dough into 1 or 2 smooth cakes, one just slightly larger than the other if you are making a double-crust pie. Roll out the dough and place it in the pan as directed in the recipe of your choice. Put the pie shell in the freezer and let it rest for at least 30 minutes before baking.

TO FULLY BAKE A PIE SHELL

Preheat an oven to 400°F (200°C). Line the pie shell with aluminum foil and fill with dried beans or pie weights. Bake for 10 minutes, then lower the heat to 350°F (180°C) and continue baking until the shell is golden brown, about 15–20 minutes longer. Remove the weights and aluminum foil during the last 5 minutes of baking. Let cool completely on a rack.

Baguette; Country Bread; Basic Pie Pastry

ROASTING & CARVING

Moist and tender whole roast poultry, prime rib of beef, or leg of lamb makes a magnificent main course for any festive dinner party. Follow the guidelines below to help you achieve the best results.

Bear in mind that roasts put into the oven straight from the refrigerator will take longer to cook, so it's best to let the meat stand at room temperature for about 1 hour before roasting. After roasting, and when done to your liking, let roasts rest at room temperature, loosely covered with aluminum foil, for about 15 mintues before carving. Be sure to allow enough time to cook the roast and let it stand before carving so that dinner is not delayed.

Roasting Prime Rib of Beef

Preheat an oven to 500°F (260°C). Place the prime rib roast, ribside down, in a roasting pan and roast it for 15 minutes.

• Reduce the heat to 325°F (165°C) and continue roasting until the meat is browned and reaches the desired degree of doneness.

• For rare beef, remove the roast when an instant-read thermometer inserted into the center of the meat, not touching the bone, registers 120°F (50°C), about 15 minutes per pound (500 g). For medium beef, remove when the temperature registers 135°F (57°C), about 20 minutes per pound (500 g).

• Let the roast rest for 15 minutes before carving. This will allow the meat to reabsorb its juices, and it will also continue to cook, adding 5°–7°F (2°–3°C) to the final temperature.

CARVING PRIME RIB OF BEEF

A prime rib is fairly simple to carve, provided you have a large, sharp knife for slicing and a sturdy fork to steady the roast. Serve some slices still attached to the ribs for guests who like the bones.

1 To cut the first slice, place the roast, ribs down, on a sturdy carving surface and steady it by inserting a carving fork into the top. Cut a vertical slice against the grain down to the rib bone; cut along the bone to free the slice.

2 Continue carving. Cutting parallel to the first slice, continue to carve slices of the desired thickness. As individual bones are exposed, cut between them to remove them, or leave them attached to a slice for guests who request them.

Roasting Leg of Lamb

Preheat an oven to 350°F (180°C). Place the lamb on a rack in a roasting pan and roast in the oven until it is browned.

• For rare to medium-rare lamb, remove from the oven when an instant-read thermometer inserted into the thickest part, not touching the bone, registers 135°–140°F (57°–60°C), about 1½ hours for a 6–7-lb (3–3.5-kg) leg. For medium lamb, remove when the temperature registers 150°F (65°C), about 2 hours.

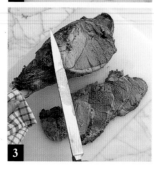

CARVING LEG OF LAMB

Shaped like an irregular, elongated pear, a leg of lamb presents a bit of a challenge to the carver. The keys to successfully carving the leg lie in cutting parallel to the bone and providing each guest with slices from both sides of the leg.

1 Slice the rounded side of the leg. Grasp the end of the shank bone with a kitchen towel and tilt it slightly upward. Carve a slice from the rounded outer side of the leg at its widest point, cutting away from you and parallel to the bone.

2 Cut parallel slices. Cutting parallel to the first slice, continue carving the meat in thin slices until you have cut enough to serve each guest a slice.

3 Carve the inner side of the leg. Rotate the leg of lamb to expose the inner side of the leg, which is slightly more tender. Still cutting parallel to the bone, carve one slice of meat for each guest.

Roasting Chicken

Preheat an oven to 325°F (165°C). Place the chicken on its side on a rack in a roasting pan.

• Roast the chicken until golden brown. Turn it to the other side at even intervals during cooking, finishing it breast-side up.

• Remove the chicken from the oven when an instant-read thermometer inserted into the thickest part of the thigh, not touching the bone, registers 180°F (82°C). See at right above for roasting times.

ROASTING TIME IN HOURS

For a stuffed bird, add 30–45 minutes to the total roasting time.

	2–4 lb (1–2 kg)	4–7 lb (2–3.5 kg)	8–12 lb (4–6 kg)	12–16 lb (6–8 kg)	16–20 lb (8–10 kg)
Turkey			2–3¼	3¼–4¼	4¼–5
Chicken	1–1½	1½–2			

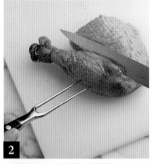

CARVING CHICKEN

Carving a chicken is similar to carving a turkey. But because the bird is smaller, you may use a smaller knife, which is easier to handle. The breast can be removed in several slices, as for turkey, or in one piece.

1 Remove the leg and the wing. Cut through the skin between the leg and breast to locate the thigh joint; cut through the joint to sever the leg (shown at left). Cut through the shoulder joint where it meets the breast to remove the wing.

2 Separate the drumstick and thigh. If the chicken is small, serve the whole leg as one portion. If it is large, cut through the joint to separate the drumstick and thigh into two pieces.

3 Carve the breast. Starting at the breastbone, cut downward and parallel to the rib cage, carving the meat into long, thin slices. Or, cut away the meat from the breastbone in one piece and then slice.

Roasting Turkey

Preheat an oven to 350°F (180°C). Place the turkey, breast-side down, on a rack in a roasting pan and tent loosely with foil.

• Place the turkey in the oven and roast, turning it breast-side up for the last 45 minutes of cooking, until it is golden brown all over. Using an instant-read thermometer, insert into the thickest part of the thigh, making sure not to touch the bone. It should register 180°F (82°C). See table above for roasting times.

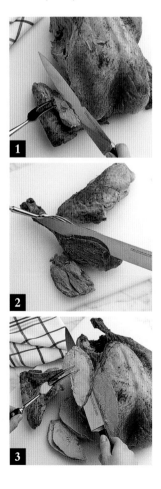

CARVING TURKEY

Use a slicing knife with a long, flexible, but sturdy blade. Carve only as much meat as you need to serve at one time, completing one side of the turkey before starting the next.

1 Remove the leg and the wing. Cut through the skin between the leg and breast to locate the thigh joint; cut through the joint to sever the leg. To remove the wing (shown at left), cut through the shoulder joint where it meets the breast.

2 Slice the drumstick and thigh. Cut through the joint to separate the drumstick and thigh. Serve them whole or carve them, cutting the meat into thin slices parallel to the bone.

3 Carve the breast. Starting at the breastbone, cut downward and parallel to the rib cage, carving the meat into long, thin slices. Or, cut away the meat from the breastbone in one piece and then slice.

SETTING A TABLE

The tableware you select will vary with the menu, style and level of formality you desire. An informal setting draws on all-purpose, everyday pieces. A formal setting employs more varied and elegant tableware.

Whatever kind of table you set, some basic rules govern its arrangement. Plates, glasses, knives, forks and spoons are all placed with efficiency in mind, each set in the most convenient spot for your guests.

Logic lies behind the rules of serving and clearing. Food is always passed or served to each guest's left-hand side and cleared from the right.

All-Purpose Glass

Informal Setting

The setting shown at right is simple and informal in two basic ways. First, it uses everyday tableware (in this case, three pieces of stainless-steel flatware), a country-style pottery plate, a cotton napkin and an all-purpose glass.

More significantly, the setting reflects the simplicity of the meal to come. A small fork awaits a first-course salad, to be followed by a main course for which the larger fork and the knife will be used. The single all-purpose glass indicates that one kind of wine, or perhaps water or some other nonalcoholic beverage, will be poured.

Some general lessons for setting any informal table may be readily drawn from this basic arrangement. All implements are placed in the order in which they will be used. The napkin goes to the left of the plate and forks, its folded side facing the plate, ready to be picked up by a corner, opened and placed in the lap when a guest sits down. Next comes the first-course fork, then the dinner fork, closest to the plate.

The dinner knife goes to the right of the plate, its blade facing inward, ready for the guest to pick it up for cutting. If soup were planned as a preliminary course, its spoon would be placed just to the right of the knife, since most people eat soup with their right hand. The glass is positioned above and just inside the knife, within easy reach but well clear of cutlery and plates.

Other implements are notable by their absence. For an informal meal, dessert forks or spoons arrive at the table with that course, placed on the side of each plate. Likewise, teaspoons are offered only when coffee is passed, placed on the side of each saucer, thus avoiding unnecessary table clutter earlier in the meal.

Whatever informal setting you arrange, you might also want to consider using place mats. They not only protect an attractive table, but also highlight each individual setting and add to the ambience with their color or pattern.

Napkin

Salad Fork / Dinner Fork   *Dinner Plate*   *Dinner Knife*

Additional flatware that could supplement the standard pieces used in the place settings on these pages includes, from left to right: luncheon fork; luncheon knife; fish fork; fish knife, which also may be used for butter service; round-bowl spoon for cream soups; oval-bowl spoon for other soups; serving fork; serving spoon; slicer/server for appetizers, main courses or desserts.

Formal Setting

This setting reflects the elegant style of a formal meal. Fine china is complemented by silver flatware, an embroidered linen napkin and cut-crystal glasses with gold rims. Match with a linen tablecloth or, if the table's surface is beautiful in its own right, it could be left bare.

Each item is carefully positioned in the order in which it will be used. The rectangular napkin is on the far left, ready to be unfolded and placed in the lap; a more elaborate fold such as one of those shown on pages 182–183 might be placed in the center of the dinner plate.

To the right of the napkin go the forks, arranged left to right in their order of use. Above the forks, a small plate awaits bread, with an individual butter knife laid across the top rim with its handle pointing to the right, since most people will pick it up with their right hand.

The dinner knife, as always, goes just to the right of the plate, its blade facing inward. A soup spoon to the right of the knife indicates that soup will be served.

Glassware should also be arranged in order of use. Within closest reach of the right hand is a glass for the white wine that is usually poured with first courses. To its left, a larger glass awaits the red wine that would be poured next. Above both glasses goes an even larger goblet for guests who might request water.

In a formal setting such as this, dessert utensils may be placed on the table before the meal, just above the dinner plate. Logic, again, determines their exact positioning: The dessert spoon's handle faces right, since most guests are likely to pick it up with their right hand, and the fork's handle points to the left, to be picked up easily with the left hand. Alternatively, the utensils could be placed on the sides of the dessert plates when they are served.

Depending on your own formal menu, you can further elaborate the setting. Many different shapes and sizes of glasses and table utensils have evolved over the centuries; some of the most common appear in the boxes at left and right. But while their combination of elegance and functionality is appealing, such items are not absolutely essential to a formal menu. Any table set with simplicity, order and, above all, a regard for the convenience and comfort of your guests will be elegant.

Water Goblet

Bread Plate / Butter Knife

Red Wineglass

White Wineglass

Dessert Spoon / Dessert Fork

Napkin

Salad Fork / Dinner Fork

Dinner Plate

Dinner Knife / Soup Spoon

For either red or white wine, fill the glass two-thirds full. Champagne flutes can be slightly fuller. Specialized glassware, distinguished by its shape, includes, from left to right: narrow glass for white wine; rounded glass for Burgundy or other red wines; oversized balloon glass for red or white wine, or water; all-purpose wineglass; snifter for Cognac or brandy; Champagne flute; sherry or dessert wineglass.

NAPKIN FOLDING

A napkin folded into one of the five simple, classic patterns shown here can add variety and style to any party table.

We recommend using sturdy-weave cotton or linen, which is more absorbent and soil-resistant than synthetic or coated fabrics. For the crispest folds, iron the napkins first; you may also want to apply a light spray starch. A final decorative touch such as ribbon, twine, string or flowers adds extra charm.

For clarity, the illustrations here use a plain 20-inch-square (50-cm) linen napkin. But feel free to choose any fabric, color, pattern and size that suits the setting and mood of your party.

Bow Tie

This easiest of folds has universal appeal, appearing in many of the menus in this book. As effortless in effect as it is quickly achieved, the bow tie works well with napkins of any fabric or size. This fold is ideal with a casual setting or even on a semi-formal table.

For a striking effect, use this fold for such unconventional napkins as Western-style bandanas or large swatches of Indian madras cotton. You may also want to tuck little gifts inside the knots, such as the miniature rolling pins shown in the Indian Summer Brunch on page 75, to add an amusing touch that carries out the theme or ambience of your party.

1

2

1 Fold the upper left corner of the napkin to the lower right corner, forming a triangle.

2 Rotate so the tip faces you. Roll up from the bottom to form a cylinder.

3 Tie a knot in the center. Adjust the ends and knot to form a V shape or drape diagonally across a plate.

3

Astoria

This simple fold achieves a graceful effect suitable for both informal and elegant settings. For an attractive variation, omit folding down the top point in Step 2 to make a napkin with points at both ends.

1

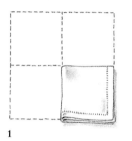

2

3

4

1 Fold the napkin into quarters by first folding down the top half, then folding the leftside over the right.

2 Rotate 90 degrees so the open end points toward you. Fold the top point down to the center.

3 Fold in the left corner so its point reaches just past the center.

4 Cross the right corner just over the left and carefully turn the napkin over.

Bishop's Hat

The bishop's hat has adorned fine tables for centuries and lends distinction to today's more formal occasions. You can present it either standing up or lying flat.

1 Starting with a triangle, hold your finger at the center of the long side and fold the right corner up to the top corner; then fold the left corner up to the top corner.

2 Fold the bottom corner up to within 1 inch (2.5 cm) of the top corner; then fold the bottom corner back down to touch the bottom edge.

3 Carefully turn the napkin over and fold the left side into the center.

4 Fold the right side into the center, tucking its point into the previous fold. Turn the napkin over again.

Buffet Server

Both attractive and useful, this fold yields a decorative napkin that conveniently holds an individual set of flatware for guests helping themselves to food.

1 Fold the napkin into quarters, rotating it so the open points are at the top.

2 Fold the point of the topmost layer down to meet the bottom corner, forming a pocket.

3 Fold the left and right corners underneath. Tuck cutlery inside the pocket.

The Fan

Use the fan for a festive table, like the one set for the Heritage Christmas menu (page 145). To stiffen the napkin, iron the pleats.

1 Fold the napkin in half vertically. From the bottom, fold back and forth into ½-inch (12-mm) accordion pleats, stopping when the unfolded portion is half as tall as it is wide.

2 Fold the napkin in half with the pleats on the outside.

3 Fold all the layers of the top square in half diagonally, tucking the point under the pleats. Lift the napkin from the right side so it stands up and the pleats fan out.

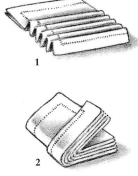

FLOWER ARRANGING

Examples of casual, easily achieved flower arrangements may be found in almost every menu section of this book. For some festive occasions, you may want more elaborate decorations of the kind you would order from a professional florist. However, here we present three simple arrangements that can be done at home with lovely results. All that's required is a little time, imagination and patience, as well as the assistance of simple tools and materials that can be found at a variety store, florist's supplier or hardware store.

Festive Arrangement

Equally at home as a centerpiece or on a side table, this all-purpose arrangement may be created with a wide variety of flowers and greens. For the version shown here, we selected an array of white blossoms and delicate greenery: tulips, hyacinths, lilies of the valley, snowballs and ferns. You could vary the elements with your own favorite flowers in any pleasing combination.

To prepare this arrangement, you will need a container with a wide mouth and low base; a chunk of florist's foam cut to fit the container; and florist's tape. At your flower shop, select 8–10 green fronds; about two dozen sturdy blossoms; and about a dozen each of two or more kinds of more delicate flowers. Use flower shears to cut all stems diagonally and put the flowers in warm water until ready to use; soak the foam in warm water for 30 minutes before using.

1 Secure the florist's foam in place in the container with strips of florist's tape.

2 Create a fringe of ferns, inserting the stems around the base of the foam. Evenly insert less expensive, sturdy-stemmed flowers (we used tulips).

3 Fill in the gaps by irregularly distributing more expensive blooms (here, snowballs and hyacinths). Finish with delicate flowers such as lilies of the valley.

Basic flower-arranging equipment (clockwise from top left):
1 Florist's tape, *for wrapping fragile stems, binding flowers together and strapping down florist's foam.*
2 Florist's foam, *or oasis, to be cut to fit into a bowl, soaked in water and used as a base into which flower stems are pushed.*
3 Frogs, *spiked metal disks into which stem or branch ends may be pushed to secure them.*
4 Chicken wire, *available in hardware stores, for use inside a bowl as a mesh to support branches and stems.*
5 Clippers, *to cut thicker stems or branches.*
6 Shears, *for cutting flower stems.*
7 Gardening gloves, *for handling thorny or prickly flowers.*
8 Florist's wire, *ranging from thin to thick gauges, used for reinforcing stems or binding them together.*

Rose Braid

A special occasion becomes even more memorable when decorated with roses. To give even more elegance to a rose bouquet, you could add a braid that cascades down the side of the vase.

You'll need about four dozen roses in all. Depending on the style of your party, choose either a mix of colors or blossoms of a single hue. If you plan to use hot-house roses, buy them two days ahead of time so they can unfurl a bit. An urn-shaped vase will complement the elegance of the bouquet and provide height to lift the braid. Cut a piece of florist's foam to fit the container and presoak it in warm water for 30 minutes; place it inside the vase and add water. Arrange about three dozen of the roses, ends trimmed, in a bouquet shape and fill in any gaps with small roses or tight buds.

To prepare the braid, select about 15 roses, in an even range of blossom sizes from small to large. Trim all their stems to a uniform 6-inch (15-cm) length. Place the roses in warm water until ready to use. As a base for the braid, use two 18-inch-long (45-cm) strips of variegated ivy. If you like, you could make the braid longer, buying about a dozen more roses for each additional foot in length. Use both florist's tape and thin florist's wire to secure the arrangement.

1 Hold the two 18-inch-long (45-cm) strands of ivy parallel to one another. At one end, attach three small partially opened roses with 6-inch (15-cm) stems, wrapping florist's wire around the stems and ivy. Trim the rose stems to 1 inch (2.5 cm) past the wire.

2 Continue attaching bunches of three roses, using the blossoms to conceal the wire of the previous bunch. Use fuller roses as you progress from beginning to end. Leave 5 inches (12.5 cm) of ivy bare at the end.

3 Tuck the ends of the bare ivy into the vase, sticking it into the florist's foam, and secure the braid inside and along the rim with florist's tape.

Holiday Tree

Other attractive objects besides flowers make excellent candidates for festive arrangements. This centerpiece presents a tree-shaped composition of vegetables and fruits—an arrangement similar to the fruit tree in the Christmas dinner on page 147. You can give your imagination free rein when planning a holiday tree's elements, selecting from a wide range of foods and other materials and opting for either a monochromatic or varied color scheme.

A 12-inch (30-cm) Styrofoam cone serves as the base for the tree, with wooden toothpicks used as fasteners. Because foods arranged in this way will not keep long, assemble the tree the day of the party.

1 Insert wooden toothpicks into the largest items, such as limes or brussel sprouts, and attach them to the base of the cone in several layers.

2 Fill gaps with smaller items, such as broccoli, skewering them on toothpicks or, in the case of stringbeans, insert directly into the foam.

3 Top the tree with an attractive object such as a small artichoke. Add final decorations by skewering them onto toothpicks so that they rest atop the other items.

GLOSSARY

The following pages describe special ingredients and techniques used throughout the recipes in this book.

AL DENTE
An Italian term, meaning "to the tooth," used to describe the ideal degree of doneness for vegetables or cooked pasta—tender, but still firm to the bite.

ALMONDS
See *nuts*.

AQUAVIT
A clear, dry Scandinavian spirit distilled either from potatoes or grains and usually flavored with caraway, or sometimes with citrus and spices.

ARMAGNAC
A dry brandy, similar to Cognac, distilled in the Armagnac region of southwestern France from wine produced there. If unavailable, other good-quality dry wine–based brandies may be substituted.

ARUGULA
A green leaf vegetable with slender, multiple-lobed leaves that have a peppery flavor. Often used raw in salads; also known as rocket.

BELGIAN ENDIVE
A leaf vegetable with slightly bitter spear-shaped leaves, white to pale yellow–green—or sometimes red— tightly packed in cylindrical heads 4–6 inches (10–15 cm) long. Also known as chicory or witloof.

BELL PEPPERS
See *peppers*.

BREAD CRUMBS
To make fresh bread crumbs, choose a good-quality, country-style loaf made of unbleached wheat flour, with a firm, coarse crumb. Cut away the crusts and crumble the bread to the desired consistency by hand or in a blender or a food processor fitted with the metal blade.

BRUSSELS SPROUTS
Small, spherical green vegetables, usually 1–2 inches (2.5–5 cm) in diameter, resembling tiny cabbages, to which they are related.

BUTTER, CLARIFIED
Butter is often clarified—that is, its milk solids are removed— when it is to be used for cooking at higher temperatures or as a sauce. To clarify butter, melt it in a small, heavy saucepan over very low heat; watch carefully to avoid burning. Remove from the heat and let sit briefly. Then, using a spoon, skim off and discard the foam from the surface. Finally, carefully pour off the clear yellow butter, leaving the milky solids behind in the pan.

CACHACA
A smooth, colorless Brazilian rum with a strength and dryness suggestive of brandy.

CALVADOS
A dry French brandy distilled from apples and bearing the fruit's distinctive aroma and taste. Dry applejack may be substituted.

CANDY THERMOMETER
A thermometer specially designed to register temperatures in the 230°–350°F (110°–177°C) range to which sugar syrup–based mixtures are heated in dessert and candy making.

CANNING
Many of the preserves recipes in this book can be stored for long periods if they are packed into hot sterilized jars and then hot-water processed to prevent spoilage. While books on preserving will offer charts with specific times and procedures necessary to preserve different kinds of ingredients, the basic steps are as follows:

1 Thoroughly wash all jars, lids and screw bands. Place them in a large pan, add hot water to cover and bring to a full boil. Boil 10 minutes, then remove from the heat and let the jars stand in the water.

2 Using tongs, drain the jars and, while they are still hot, fill them with the preserves, leaving about ½ inch (12 mm) of head space. Gently tap and shake the jars to force out any air bubbles. Using a dampened cloth, wipe any spillage from the jar mouths, then seal the jars with the lids.

3 Meanwhile, fill a large pot with water, insert a jar rack or place a folded cloth on the bottom and bring the water to a bare simmer; bring a separate pot of water to a boil. Put the filled jars in the rack or on the cloth and add enough boiling water to cover them by at least 1 inch (2.5 cm). Return the water to a full boil, cover and begin counting processing time: 10 minutes for chutneys, jams, marmalades and conserves; 25–30 minutes for whole or halved peaches, plums and apricots.

4 Turn off the heat and remove the jars with canning tongs to a flat surface. After several hours, all of the jars should be sealed. Check the lids by touching them to see if they are concave, indicating a secure seal. If a lid is not concave, refrigerate the preserves and eat within a few weeks.

CARAWAY SEEDS
See *seeds*.

CARDAMOM
See *seeds*.

CAYENNE PEPPER
A very hot spice derived from ground dried cayenne chili peppers.

CELERIAC
Also known as celery root. The large, knobby root of a species of celery plant, with a crisp texture and flavor closely resembling the familiar stalks. Choose smaller, younger roots, to be peeled and eaten raw or cooked.

CHANTERELLES
See *mushrooms*.

CHESTNUTS
Raw chestnuts have glossy brown shells and a dark fuzzy membrane beneath the shells. Both the shells and the membrane must be removed before use. Shelled whole chestnuts or chestnut pieces, dry-packed, candied or packed in water or syrup, as well as sweetened and unsweetened chestnut purées, are available in some specialty-food shops.

CHILI PEPPERS
See *peppers*.

CITRUS FRUITS
A wide variety of citrus fruits enliven festive meals. Two in particular are well worth seeking out at well-stocked food markets:

Blood Oranges are a variety of the fruit with red pulp and orange skins tinged with red. Their flavor is more pronounced than that of regular oranges, which may be substituted for blood oranges.

Meyer Lemons are slightly larger and have thinner skins than common lemons, and they have a more pronounced, slightly sweeter aroma and taste. A mixture of 2 parts fresh lemon juice to 1 part fresh orange juice may be substituted for Meyer lemon juice in some recipes.

Sectioning Citrus Fruit
Some recipes call for segments, or sections, of citrus fruit, free of pith, peel and membranes.

1 To section a citrus fruit, first use a small, sharp knife to cut a thick slice off its bottom and top, exposing the fruit beneath the peel. Then, steadying the fruit on a work surface, thickly slice off the peel in strips, cutting off the white pith with it.

2 Hold the peeled fruit in one hand over a bowl to catch the juices. Using the same knife, carefully cut on each side of the membrane to free each section, letting the sections drop into the bowl as they are cut.

CIPOLLINE
Cipolline are small, flat, brown-skinned onions, prized in Italy for their sweetness; available in some vegetable markets, they may be replaced with pearl onions.

CLAMS
Bivalve mollusks prized for their sweet, tender flesh. Sold live in their shells, or sometimes already shucked, in fish markets or good-quality food markets with seafood departments. Check all the clams and discard any whose shells do not close tightly to the touch.

COCONUT
To toast flaked coconut, spread it evenly on a baking sheet and bake in a 350°F (180°C) oven, stirring once or twice, until pale gold, 10–20 minutes.

COGNAC
A dry spirit distilled from wine and, strictly speaking, produced in the Cognac region of France. Other good-quality dry wine–based brandies may be substituted.

CORIANDER
See *seeds.*

CORN, SWEET
Before use, fresh sweet corn must be stripped of its green outer husks and the fine inner silky threads must be removed. If a recipe calls for removing the raw kernels from an ear of corn, hold the ear by its stalk end, steadying its other end on a cutting board. With the ear at a 45-degree angle to the board, use a sharp, sturdy knife to cut down and away from you along the ear, stripping off the kernels from the cob. Continue, turning the ear with each cut.

CORNICHONS
French-style sour pickles made from gherkin cucumbers, no more than 2 inches (5 cm) in length, available in specialty-food stores.

CRAB
Already-cooked crab meat is widely available in fish markets or the seafood counters in most food markets. Most often, it has been frozen; for best flavor and texture, seek out fresh crab meat. When crab is in season, fish markets will often sell crabs boiled or steamed whole; ask for them to be cracked, so that you can open the shells by hand and remove the meat.

CUMIN
See *seeds.*

CURRANTS, DRIED
Produced from a variety of small grapes known as Zante, these dried fruits resemble tiny raisins but have a stronger, tarter flavor. Sold in the baking section of food markets. If they are unavailable, substitute raisins.

EMMENTHALER
A variety of Swiss cheese with a firm, smooth texture, large holes and a mellow, slightly sweet, nutty flavor.

FENNEL SEEDS
See *seeds.*

FETA
A white, salty, sharp-tasting cheese made from sheep or goat's milk and with a crumbly, creamy-to-dry consistency. Greek in origin.

FIGS
Summer fruit characterized by their many tiny edible seeds, sweet, slightly astringent flavor and soft, succulent texture. It is best to buy fresh figs ripe and use them immediately.

FILO
Tissue-thin sheets of flour-and-water pastry. The name derives from the Greek word for leaf. Usually found in the freezer case of a food market, or purchased fresh in Greek and Middle Eastern delicatessens; defrost frozen filo in the refrigerator thoroughly before use. As you work with the filo, cover the unused sheets with a very lightly dampened kitchen towel to keep them from drying out.

GINGER
The rhizome of the tropical ginger plant, which yields a sweet, strong-flavored spice. Whole ginger may be purchased fresh in a well-stocked food shop or vegetable market. Ginger pieces are available crystallized or candied, or preserved in syrup. Ground dried ginger is easily found in the food market spice section.

GOAT CHEESE
Any of a number of cheeses made from goat's milk; also commonly known by the French word *chèvre.* Most goat cheeses are fresh and creamy, with a distinctively sharp tang; they usually are sold shaped into rounds or logs.

GRAPE LEAVES
In Greek and other Middle Eastern cuisines, grapevine leaves are commonly used as edible wrappers. If fresh leaves are available, wash them thoroughly before use. Bottled leaves, available in ethnic delicatessens and the specialty-food section of well-stocked food markets, should be gently rinsed of their brine.

EGGS
Some recipes in this book call for the use of raw eggs. It is advised that pregnant women, very young children, and individuals with poor immune responses should avoid consuming these recipes.

Whisking Egg Whites
1 Put the whites into a large bowl with a pinch of cream of tartar. With a wire balloon whisk, or an electric beater set on medium speed, beat the whites with broad, sweeping strokes to incorporate as much air as possible. As the whites begin to thicken and turn a glossy, snowy white, lift out the whisk or beater: If a soft peak forms, then droops back on itself, the whites have reached the "soft peak" stage.

2 For the "stiff peak" stage, continue beating until the whites form stiff, unmoving moist peaks when the whisk or beaters are lifted straight out.

Whisking Egg Yolks with Sugar
Put the egg yolks and sugar into a large bowl, place the bowl in hot water and beat until warm to the touch. Remove from the hot water and, with a wire whisk or an electric beater set on high speed, beat until thick and pale, about 8 minutes. To test if beaten sufficiently, lift out the whisk or beater: The mixture should flow in a ribbon that takes about 3 seconds to fall back onto the surface and then slowly dissolve.

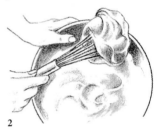

GRUYÈRE
A variety of Swiss cheese with a firm, smooth texture, small holes and a strong, tangy flavor.

HAZELNUTS
See *nuts.*

HOT-WATER PROCESSING
See *canning.*

JALAPEÑO CHILIES
See *peppers.*

JULIENNE
Refers both to cutting food into long, thin strips and to the strips themselves. To julienne vegetables, thinly slice lengthwise, then stack several slices and slice again into thin strips; alternatively, use a mandoline or the julienne-cutting disk of a food processor.

LEMONS, MEYER
See *citrus fruits.*

LEMON VERBENA

A strongly lemon-scented herb, native to South America. Available in some fruit and vegetable markets, or you can grow your own.

MADEIRA

A sweet, amber-colored dessert wine originating on the Portuguese island of Madeira.

MARSALA

A dry or sweet amber Italian wine from the area of Marsala, in Sicily;

widely used to flavor meats, poultry, vegetables and desserts.

MASCARPONE

A thick Italian cream cheese, usually sold in tubs and similar to French crème fraîche. Look for mascarpone in the cheese case of an Italian delicatessen or a specialty-food shop.

MOZZARELLA

A rindless white, mild-tasting Italian cheese. Look for fresh mozzarella sold immersed in water.

LOBSTER

Although many seafood stores and some food markets sell lobsters already cooked, cleaned and shelled, it is usually far more economical, and yields better results, to buy a live lobster and cook it yourself.

To Remove Lobster Meat

1 After cooking a whole lobster as specified in the recipe, let it rest until cool enough to handle. Then, steadying the body with one hand, firmly grasp a claw where it joins the body; twist and pull to remove it. Repeat with the other claw.

2 To enable the claw meat to be extracted, crack its shell with a lobster cracker or mallet. Peel away the shell and gently remove the meat, taking care to keep it in one piece if possible. Twist and pull off the four small legs arrayed along each side of the body.

3 To split the lobster in half, turn it underside up on the work surface. Steadying it with one hand, use a large, sharp knife to cut through the soft shell from head to tail. Continue cutting through the head and tail sections and downward through the harder shell along the back. If a black vein is visible along the center of the tail meat, remove and discard.

4 Using a small, sharp-edged spoon, scoop out the stomach sac and other soft matter from the head portion of the shell halves. Using a fork, spear one end of the tail meat and gently pull it out of the shell. If the recipe requires the shell halves for presentation, clean and reserve them.

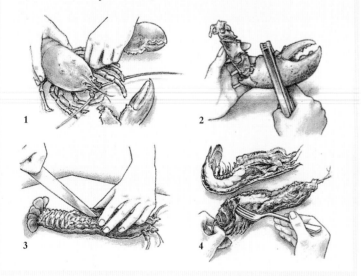

MUSHROOMS

Cultivated white and brown mushrooms are available in food markets and fruit and vegetable markets. Porcini, the widely used Italian term for *Boletus edulis*, are popular wild mushrooms with a rich, meaty flavor; also known by the French term *cèpe*, they are most commonly sold in dried form in Italian delicatessens and specialty-food shops, and are reconstituted in liquid to use. Chanterelles (shown above), subtly flavored, pale yellow, trumpet-shaped wild mushrooms about 2–3 inches (5–7.5 cm) in length, are also cultivated commercially, and may be found in specialty-food markets and fruit and vegetable stores.

MUSSELS

Before cooking, these bluish black–shelled bivalves require special cleaning. Rinse the mussels thoroughly under cold running water. One at a time, hold them under the water and scrub with a firm-bristled brush to remove any stubborn dirt. Firmly grasp the fibrous beard attached to the side of each mussel and pull it off. Discard any mussels whose shells do not close tightly to the touch.

NUTS

To toast almonds, hazelnuts, pecans, pine nuts and walnuts, preheat an oven to 325°F (165°C). Spread the nuts in a single layer on a sided baking sheet and toast in the oven until they begin to change color, 5–10 minutes. Remove from the oven and let cool to room temperature. Toasting also loosens the skins of hazelnuts and walnuts, which may be removed by wrapping the still-warm nuts in a cotton towel and rubbing against them with the palms of your hands.

To chop nuts, spread them in a single layer on a nonslip cutting surface. Using a chef's knife, carefully chop the nuts with a gentle rocking motion. Alternatively, put a handful or two of nuts in a food processor fitted with the metal blade and use a few rapid on-off pulses to chop the nuts to desired consistency; repeat with the

remaining nuts in batches. Be careful not to process the nuts too long, or their oils will be released and the nuts will turn into a paste.

OILS

Extra-virgin olive oil, extracted from olives on the first pressing without use of heat or chemicals, is preferred for most recipes in this book. Many brands, varying in color and strength of flavor, are available; choose one that suits your taste. Pure olive oil, derived from the later pressings, has less of the fruit's distinctive flavor and may be used for sautéing and frying, or to mix with extra-virgin oil in salad dressings for a milder flavor. Walnut oil has a rich, nutty taste prized in dressings; that made from toasted nuts has the deepest color and fullest flavor.

OLIVES

Ripe black olives are cured in combinations of salt, seasonings, brines, vinegars and oils to produce pungently flavored results. Good-quality cured olives, such as Niçoise, Moroccan, or Kalamata varieties, are available in specialty-food shops and well-stocked food markets.

ORANGE FLOWER WATER

A sweet, aromatic essence distilled from the natural oils present in orange petals and used as a subtle flavoring in Middle Eastern and other cuisines.

ORANGES, BLOOD

See *citrus fruits*.

OYSTERS

Always buy fresh oysters from a reputable fish market. They vary in size from area to area. They are available live in the shell as well as shucked and in their liquor.

PANCETTA

Italian-style unsmoked bacon cured with salt, pepper, and other spices. Available in Italian markets and specialty-food stores.

PARMESAN CHEESE

A hard, thick-crusted Italian cow's milk cheese with a sharp, salty, full flavor. Buy in block form, to grate fresh. The finest Italian variety is designated Parmigiano-Reggiano.

PEPPERS

Widely varied in shape, size and hue, and ranging in taste from mild and sweet to fiery hot, peppers add flavor, color and texture to savory recipes.

Bell Peppers, also known as capsicums, have a sweet, mild taste and a bell shape; they come in a range of colors and flavors.

Chili Peppers include a wide variety of peppers prized for the mild-to-hot spiciness they impart as a seasoning. Red ripe chilies are sold fresh and dried. Fresh green chilies include the mild-to-hot dark green poblano; the long, mild Anaheim, New Mexico or green chili; and small, fiery serranos and jalapeños. When handling most chili peppers, it is advisable to wear rubber gloves to prevent your skin from coming into contact with the pepper's volatile oils.

To Roast, Peel and Derib Peppers

1 When a recipe calls for roasted peppers, there are several ways to achieve this. One method is to spear each pepper individually on a long fork and hold it directly over an open flame, turning until the skin is evenly blackened. Alternatively, place the whole peppers on a baking sheet and roast in a 400°F (200°C) oven, or under a broiler (griller), turning occasionally with tongs, until the skins are evenly blackened.

2 After roasting, place the peppers in a paper bag or plastic container and let them sit until cool enough to handle, about 10 minutes. When cool, use your fingers to peel off the charred skins. Cut the peppers in half and pull out and discard the stems, seeds and ribs. Then use the peppers as directed in the recipe.

PEARS

Several pear varieties are available each season. Comice pears (above left) are large, with short necks and greenish skin highlighted with a red blush; they are excellent for eating and in desserts. Bartlett pears (above middle), also called Williams' pears, are fine-textured, juicy and mild; they are equally good for cooking or eating. Long, slender, tapered Bosc pears (above right), with their yellow and russet skins and slightly grainy, solid-textured flesh, are good for cooking.

PECANS
See *nuts*.

PINE NUTS
See *nuts*.

POLENTA
Coarsely but evenly ground yellow cornmeal. Available in Italian grocers or some well-stocked food shops.

PORCINI
See *mushrooms*.

POUSSIN
A small, immature chicken, weighing no more than about 1 pound (500 g), prized for its tender, sweet flesh.

PROSCIUTTO
Italian raw ham, a specialty of Parma, cured by dry-salting, then air-drying for half a year or longer. Usually cut into tissue-thin slices to eat.

QUAIL
A small game bird, usually a single serving, with moist, tender, very flavorful dark meat.

SAFFRON
Saffron threads are the dried stigmas of a species of the crocus flower. It is used to perfume and color many classic Mediterranean and East Indian dishes. Look for products labeled "pure saffron." Saffron threads have more flavor and should be crushed before use: First, put them in a metal kitchen spoon and hold the spoon over a hot burner for a few seconds; then use the back of a teaspoon to crush the threads, or pulverize in a mortar with a pestle.

SCALLOPS
Bivalve mollusks that come in two common varieties: The round flesh of the sea scallop is usually 1½ inches (4 cm) in diameter, while the bay scallop is considerably smaller. Usually sold already shelled.

SEEDS
Toasting before use enriches and releases the flavor of spice seeds. To toast seeds, stir them in a small, dry heavy frying pan over moderate heat until you can smell their aroma, about 1–2 minutes. If grinding is required, let them cool slightly, then place in an electric spice mill or a clean coffee grinder and pulverize, or crush them in a mortar with a pestle.

SHERRY
Fortified, cask-aged wine, ranging from dry to sweet, enjoyed as an aperitif and used as a flavoring in both savory and sweet recipes.

SHRIMP
Fresh, raw shrimp (prawns) are usually sold with the heads already removed but the shells intact. If fresh shrimp is unavailable, frozen may be substituted.

1 To peel, with your thumbs, split open the shrimp's thin shell along the concave side, between its two rows of legs. Peel away the shell; leave the last segment with tail fin intact and attached to the meat, if desired.

2 With a small, sharp knife, carefully make a shallow slit along the peeled shrimp's back, just deep enough to expose the long, usually dark-colored, veinlike intestinal tract. With the tip of the knife or your fingers, lift up and pull out the vein, discarding it.

SQUAB
A delicate-flavored, tender pigeon raised specifically for the table. Dark and rich, the meat can be compared to duck. The single-serving birds, usually weighing about 1 pound (500 g), are available either fresh or frozen from good-quality butchers.

STAR ANISE
Not to be confused with aniseed. Star anise is a small, hard, brown seedpod resembling an eight-pointed star, used whole or broken into individual points to lend its distinctive anise flavor to savory or sweet dishes.

TOMATOES
During summer, when tomatoes are in season, choose heirloom tomatoes when available. They can usually be found at local farmers markets. Other large beefsteak tomatoes have a robust flavor and meaty texture to match their name. Bite-sized cherry tomatoes are prized for their sweet flavor and juiciness. Plum tomatoes, sometimes called Roma or egg tomatoes, are likely to have the best flavor and texture when other tomatoes are not at the peak of season. Whole, crushed or puréed plum tomatoes are also the best canned product, adding their rich flavor to sauces, braises and stews; look for good-quality imported Italian brands.

TOMATOES, SUN-DRIED
When dried in the sun, tomatoes develop an intense, sweet-tart flavor and a pleasantly chewy texture. Available either packed in oil or packaged dry in specialty-food shops.

TOMATO PURÉE
Good-quality canned tomato purées are available in most food markets. To make your own tomato purée, peel and seed the tomatoes, then purée in a blender or a food processor.

WALNUT OIL
See *oils*.

WALNUTS
See *nuts*.

ZEST
The brightly colored, outermost layer of a citrus fruit's peel, the zest, contains most of the fruit's flavorful oils. The zest can be removed with a simple tool known as a zester by drawing its sharp-edged holes across the fruit's skin to remove the zest in thin strips, or by using the fine holes on a handheld grater. Alternatively, remove strips of zest with a vegetable peeler, taking care not to remove any white pith. Thinly slice the strips with a small, sharp knife.

INDEX

ACKNOWLEDGMENTS

The publishers would like to thank the following people and organizations for their assistance and support in producing this book. For their generosity in lending props and providing supplies: Beaver Bros. Antiques, Michelle Carrara, Janice Nicks Fisher, Iris Fuller and her team, the staff at Green Valley Growers, Stephen Griswold, Sue Fisher King, Dennis Leggett, Silver Terrace Nurseries, D.D. Stoner, Alta Tingle at The Gardener and Chuck Williams. For their help with the manuscript and design: Carrie Bradley, Kimberly Chun, Ken DellaPenta, Jody Ginsberg, Jonathan Kauffman, Lynn Meinhardt, Jonathan Schwartz, Sharon Silva, Juli Vendzules and Steven Wooster. For their photo assistance: Susanna Allen, Daniel Becker, Mark Eakle, and Sharon C. Lott.

For their generosity, we also thank Bob Long and Pat Perini of Long Vineyards, the Niebaum-Coppola Estate, and Jane and John Weil. Special thanks to Dan Glazier, Mr. and Mrs. J. Van Lott, Jennifer Millar, Mr. and Mrs. John B. Ritchie, and the staff at Square One Restaurant.

The following provided the use of their homes and property as settings for this book: Joyce Goldstein, Richard and Ann Grace of Grace Family Vineyards, Eric and Kaye Herbranson, Sue Fisher King, Mary and Howard Lester, Edward and Cynthia Mackay, Ken Monnens, Robert Cave-Rogers, Chuck Williams, and Paul Vincent Wiseman.

Published in the U.S.A. by
Weldon Owen Inc.
814 Montgomery Street
San Francisco, CA 94133

In collaboration with Williams-Sonoma
3250 Van Ness Avenue, San Francisco, CA 94109

The Williams-Sonoma Entertaining Series
conceived and produced by Weldon Owen Inc.

WILLIAMS-SONOMA
Founder and Vice-Chairman: Chuck Williams

WELDON OWEN INC.
Chief Executive Officer: John Owen
President and Chief Operating Officer: Terry Newell
VP International Sales: Stuart Laurence
Creative Director: Gaye Allen
Publisher: Hannah Rahill
Associate Creative Director: Leslie Harrington
Sales Manager: Emily Jahn
Senior Designer: Charlene Charles
Assistant Editor: Donita Boles
Production: Chris Hemesath, Teri Bell
Production Coordinator: Libby Temple
Digital Production: Karen Kemp
Front and Back Cover Photography: Quentin Bacon
Front and Back Cover Food Stylist: Kevin Crafts
Front Cover Prop Stylist: Leigh Noe

Original project management by Tori Ritchie. Editorial support by Norman Kolpas, Carolyn Miller, and Janique Poncelet. Original design by John Bull. Recipe photography by Allan Rosenberg and Allen V. Lott with additional photography by Peter Johnson. Consultant styling by Sandra Griswold. Prop styling by Karen Nicks. Food styling by Susan Massey with additional food styling by Heidi Gintner, Danielle Di Salvo, and Janice Baker. Wine consulting by Evan Goldstein. Illustrations by Alice Harth.

For information about special discounts for bulk purchases, please contact Weldon Owen Inc. at info@weldonowen.com or (415) 291-0100.

This edition first published in 2004.
10 9 8 7 6 5 4 3 2 1

Library of Congress Cataloging-in-Publication Data is available.

ISBN 1 740895 20 7

Printed and bound in China by SNP Leefung Printers

A NOTE ON WEIGHTS AND MEASURES
All recipes include customary U.S., U.K. and metric measurements. Metric conversions are based on a standard developed for these books and have been rounded off. Actual weights may vary.